Open Wider the Door

*The Intersection of Kriya Yoga
and Mystical Christianity*

Isha Das

(Craig Bullock)

DEDICATION

Open Wider The Door is dedicated to my dear friend
and elder brother, Swami Nirvanananda.

CONTENTS

ACKNOWLEDGMENTS

Any noble endeavor is always the fruit of many hands and many hearts. So it is with *Open Wider the Door*.

I am grateful to my wife, Vickijo, for her constant support and love. Her grace is my inspiration, now and forever.

I am grateful to Mary McFee for all of the time she put into editing, meeting with me, and shaping my writings into this book. She brings not only tremendous talent to her work, but great love and profound insight. Mary, you are a great gift to the world. Thank you!

I am also very appreciative of the staff at The Assisi Institute, to Adam Reitz, for designing the cover of this book and all of the hard work and creativity that you bring to our mission; to Purnima, for all of your support, prayers, and commitment to the path of Kriya Yoga; and to Ursula Arnold, for all of the compassion you bring to our work, constantly reminding us that it's all about love.

Finally, I want to thank my spiritual brothers and sisters within The Assisi Institute. Together, we are furthering the work of Paramahansa Yogananda and bringing much needed light into the world. I thank God daily for all of you!

FORWARD

Jesus pointed the way beyond "spiritual materialism" when he said, "Abide in me as I abide in you. Just as the branch cannot bear fruit by itself unless it abides in the vine, neither can you unless you abide in me" (John 15:4).

Thomas Merton writes, "The spiritual life aims at "abiding," not at fruit. Fruit will flow from my awareness of the deep inner connection with the Divine reality that is my birthright. When I aim at fruit rather than 'abiding' I get neither fruit nor connection" (Thoughts in Solitude #30).

To live spiritually, to live in awareness of one's connection with the Divine, is one's birthright. However, laying claim to a spiritual life is often rooted in both sacred texts of an earlier age and the inspiring paradigms afforded by contemporary masters. While sacred texts can provide an outline for understanding the intended path, it is by relating to a qualified master (and lineage) and experientially incorporating his or her mentored practice that one's spirituality truly matures. Isha Das' overview of the path of Kriya Yoga within a Christian context serves as an orientation and an invitation to the spiritual life as taught and lived at The Assisi Institute in Rochester, NY.

For sure, there are numerous spiritual paths to realizing one's primordially divine self. Examples are the Orthodox Christian practices of Contemplative Prayer and the Ladder of the Beautitudes; the Way of

Nature in Daoism; and the Noble Eight-fold Path of Buddhism. In the west, for many hundreds of years, the esoteric practices of Christian mysticism were very rarely accessible by laypersons; even in monastic communities they were not widely practiced.

So it was a marvelous blessing that Paramahansa Yogananda, fulfilling his guru's vision, left India for America in 1920 to bring Kriya Yoga meditation practices for God-communion to Judeo-Christian America. His purpose was not to convert people to Hinduism. Indeed, Yogananda seriously studied the Christian tradition, came to love Jesus, and bequeathed a masterful verse-by-verse commentary on the four Gospels in *The Second Coming of Christ: The Resurrection of the Christ Within You*. His research reveals the hidden yoga of the Gospels that Jesus taught his closest disciples. Yogananda's life work, including the renowned *Autobiography of a Yogi*, has inspired hundreds of thousands to take up the Kriya Yoga path.

One so inspired is Isha Das, founder and director of The Assisi Institute. Isha Das' Christian background is Franciscan-Catholic. He received a master's degree in theology from the University of Notre Dame and counts the Franciscan contemplative Richard Rohr as an influential, early mentor. After reading Yogananda's *Autobiography*, Isha Das took initiation in Kriya Yoga and eventually received authorization to teach and initiate others from Roy Davis, a direct disciple of Yogananda. What sets Isha Das apart is his wholehearted devotion to Jesus and Mary, to Saints Francis and Clare, and to Yogananda and Anan-

damayi Ma. As a master of the Kriya Yoga path, he is
a channel of inspiration to others as teacher, writer,
spiritual director, friend, and mentor – fruits that
flow from his "deep inner connection with the Divine."

What makes this overview of Kriya Yoga so vital, so
effective, is Isha Das' style of communication: and, on
the other hand, the clarity and harmony of bottom-
line principles. Regarding the former, Isha Das' language is straightforward and not-so-familiar terms are
given clear exposition. More importantly, Isha Das'
discussions and illustrations draw from four rich
sources: the teachings of Jesus, Francis, and other
Christian mystics; the tradition of Kriya Yoga and
particularly the writings of Yogananda; his rich understanding of developmental psychology and extensive practice as a psychotherapist; and the turning
points in his own life-journey.

At the heart of the "marriage" of Kriya Yoga and
Mystical Christianity is what we might call an immanent view of the Divine reality. John's Gospel quotes
Jesus: "Abide in me as I abide in you." According to
Genesis, humans were created in God's "image and
likeness;" moreover, the Franciscan tradition holds
that the whole created order mirrors divine attributes.
It follows that being unaware of "deep inner connections with the Divine reality" is not due to inherent
separateness; we need not create such connections, for
they already exist! Rather, we need to get beyond our
fascination with our personalities and their emotional
and conceptual entanglements. By entering the sweet
spaciousness of meditative solitude, we can become

aware of and then cultivate our inner connections with the Divine.

The question we might well ask at the outset is one Isha Das poses in his opening chapter: How open to the transformative energy of divine love do we want to be? Isha Das writes, "The entire path of Kriya Yoga, as briefly summarized in this book, serves one ultimate purpose: to avail us of ... Bliss, of the Holy Spirit, of Divine Love. The spiritual life is simply the ever-deepening process of living a divine life, of becoming one with the force of Love."

Many who wish to live a life of love in God-communion do not see their religious institutions offering them a path of such promise. To the contrary, given common presumptions about God being "up there," they do not believe that union with God is possible in this lifetime. The principal achievement of this book is to show how, in the traditions of mystical Christianity and Kriya Yoga, human nature and divine nature are so aligned as to make their communion possible. While sustained attention is paid to the topics of meditation, prayer, and lifestyle, this book does not offer a handbook-recipe for living spiritually; rather, it opens the door to understanding what living spiritually means within the Christian tradition and why Kriya Yoga offers a path for its attainment.

Richard Riley, Ph.D.
Emeritus Professor of Philosophy, Saint Bonaventure University
President, Olean Meditation Center

PREFACE

We live a rapidly shrinking world which is troubled by dark divisiveness. If we are going to survive as a species, we must find a way to transcend our self-destructive tendencies and celebrate our common humanity. Almost a hundred years ago, a sage from the subcontinent of India arrived on American shores. His name was Paramahansa Yogananda. He did not come seeking fame or fortune, but "to inspire nations to forsake wars, race hatreds, religious sectarianism, and the boomerang evils of materialism." Yogananda rightly believed that all human beings draw their life-blood from the same divine source and that true peace can only be established to the extent that we recognize our underlying unity in God. In this context, his life's mission was to teach Kriya Yoga as an avenue to the realization of our deepest spiritual aspirations. Far from being a religion, Kriya Yoga encompasses a series of meditation practices and lifestyle recommendations that are perfectly compatible with any and all spiritual traditions. In addition, Yogananda stressed the underlying unity between the original teachings of Jesus as taught in the Gospels and those truths proclaimed in the Bhagavad Gita.

After practicing Kriya Yoga for over thirty years, I can personally attest to the efficacy of Yogananda's ministry. Paradoxically, his teachings have made me a better Christian! This book is my attempt to honor Yogananda by underscoring the essential unity between Kriya Yoga and traditional Christian mysticism. It should be noted that Yogananda had a

profound affection for Francis of Assisi, even refer-
ring to him as his patron saint. Thus, you will find in
this book many references to the life of Francis of Assisi.

In 1987, Sri Daya Mata expressed her hope that
Yogananda's message would "open wider the door" to
self and God-realization for all who would read *The
Divine Romance*, the second published volume of
Yogananda's talks. Likewise, I pray that this book,
Open Wider The Door, will illumine your mind with
the light of truth and enflame your heart with a fiery
love for God and all of God's creatures.

Isha Das (Craig Bullock)
Founder and Spiritual Director, The Assisi Institute

Open Wider
the Door

1 THE MYSTERY OF GOD

Questions are the Beginning

A number of years ago a twenty-something man made an appointment to talk to me about spiritual matters. After exchanging pleasantries, he got right to the point: "I don't know if I believe in God."

Typically, I would have responded with any number of philosophical arguments to help him "believe." But after a moment of silent prayer, an unusual question flowed spontaneously out of me: "Do you want God to exist?"

Surprised, he asked, "Are you suggesting that I talk myself into believing in God?"

I answered, "No, not at all! What I am saying is that the existence of God is obvious to anyone who is genuinely open to the possibility of God's existence. I wonder if you have mixed feelings about *wanting* God to exist or not – and maybe these mixed feelings keep you from seeing what is right in front of you. Right now, you don't have the eyes to see God."

"What kind of eyes do I need?"

"Innocent eyes, like a child's – the kind of eyes that once were able to see and experience the wonder of life."

After a long pause, he answered, "Wow, I think you're right. I don't know if I want God to exist. I don't know if I want to be that vulnerable. I guess I'm more comfortable doubting. It gives me a sense of control."

I smiled. "No, it gives you the *illusion* of control, something all of us humans love to have. I suggest that you allow yourself to honestly struggle with the question of God. Just make sure that you bring your heart and soul into it! Struggling with the question of God, when done honestly, is a spiritual practice in itself."

My young friend looked surprised. He didn't realize that even in his questioning, he was already on the spiritual path.

Before we begin to explore the interconnectedness of Kriya Yoga and mystical Christianity, let us take some time to reflect on the transcendent mystery of God. I want to do this, in part, because in my experience of teaching Kriya Yoga I have met many people who have a very distorted sense of God. At one end of the spectrum are those who see God dualistically as a kind of superhero figure who is totally separate from us. Within such a view, it is far too easy to project very human attributes onto God, such as anger, vengefulness, or fear. Some people carry fear and guilt from heavily punitive religious traditions. Others have practiced religious traditions for a lifetime, but their practices have become rote and devoid of warmth and love. Logical thinkers may find that there simply have never been explanations or paradigms which made sense. Individuals who have found a Higher Power through recovery programs yearn to find a loving face for that Power and a pathway to greater intimacy in that essential relationship. Another group of individuals, who might be younger in age, come from no spiritual or religious traditions at all and do not even know where to begin. Often, they gravitate to a popular cultural trend which reduces God to a vague cosmic force that is either indifferent to us or easily manipulated by us. This representation of God may not be frightening, but it is neither personal nor inspirational nor uplifting; it has no power to challenge us or transform our lives. As well, our understanding of God impacts every facet of our lives, because we ultimately become what we worship and what we love. But no matter where we begin, this concept is essential: Any *authentic* intuition of God necessarily evokes wonder and a deep level of loving devotion, because God is the very essence of wonder and love.

A Dynamically Immanent God

Early in our spiritual development, many of us think that spirituality is our search for the Divine, which we earnestly undertake with study, prayer, and meditation. The truth of the matter is that God always makes the first move! Our spiritual practices, disciplines, and rituals are a response to God's invitation. We do not go to the proverbial mountain; the mountain comes to us!

Yes, God makes the first move, not necessarily because we are good, but because God is good. In the Jewish scriptures, God makes himself known to Moses, who also happens to be a murderer and a fugitive. Does God chastise Moses? No! God reveals his compassion and his desire to bring about justice. God says to Moses, "I have indeed seen the misery of my people in Egypt. I have heard them crying out because of their slave drivers, and I am concerned about their suffering. So I have come down to rescue them from the hand of the Egyptians and to bring them up out of that land into a good and spacious land, a land flowing with milk and honey... So I am sending you to Pharaoh to bring my people out of Egypt."[1] The Christmas story captures the same message, only in a much more dynamic fashion. In the Christmas event God has become one of us: fully human, fully entering into human history, fully involved in all of our affairs. Jesus is described as "Emanuel," which means "God with us." Metaphorically speaking, God is more than willing to get his hands dirty! In The Bhagavad Gita we read, "Whenever virtue declines and

---

1. Exodus 3:7–10.

vice predominates, I, the Lord, incarnate as an avatar. In visible form I appear from age to age to protect the virtuous and to destroy evildoing in order to reestablish righteousness."[2] *Clearly, therefore, spirituality is not our search for God. Rather, it is making room for God's ever-present presence in the nitty-gritty affairs of our lives.* Heaven's inexhaustible energies are always available to us, dependent only on our openness, that is, our faith, our hope, and our love. The Jesuit priest and scientist Pierre Teilhard de Chardin writes, "Through fidelity we open ourselves so intimately and continuously to the wishes and good pleasure of God, that his life penetrates and assimilates ours like a fortifying bread."[3]

Perhaps a personal story will be helpful. Many years ago, long before we were married, an angel appeared in a dream to my wife Vicki. The angel instructed her to read a specific verse, Matthew 7:7, which reads, "I say to you, ask and it shall be given, seek and you shall find, knock and the door will be opened to you." Vicki thought this was strange because she had everything she needed. Yet two weeks later her 14-year-old son Evan suffered a severe spinal cord injury that left him a quadriplegic. Many times since, Vicki and her family have had to ask for God's help, which infallibly came in ways both ordinary and miraculous. As a point of clarification, though the angelic dimension is real and all sincere spiritual seekers receive help from the hidden realms, spiritual maturity is not measured by visions, dreams, or celestial manifestations. Inte-

---

2. Paramahansa Yogananda, *God Talks With Arjuna: The Bhagavad Gita*, 2nd ed. (Los Angeles, CA: Self-Realization Fellowship, 1999), 439.
3. Pierre Teilhard de Chardin, *The Divine Milieu* (New York: HarperCollins Publishers, 2001), 113.

rior peace, a sense of God's presence, a life of virtue, and love of both friends and enemies are the sure signs of authentic spirituality.

In reflecting on the immanence of God, I do not wish to minimize the presence of tragedy, darkness, and evil; they are real and often tangible. But we must remember that God's liberating presence is also real and very tangible. Every prayer uttered, every meditation offered, and every expression of love makes God's presence more palpably and dynamically alive and active in our lives.

God: Personal or Not?

One of the fundamental questions that people ask me, especially young people, is whether or not God is personal. The answer to this question presents a paradox, something we must make peace with in any discussion of God. A paradox is not a contradiction, but two different truths held together in a creative tension. Paradox keeps us from making God into our own image and simultaneously opens us to experiencing deeper and deeper levels of the Divine.

As a starting point, we have been created in God's own "image." God created us as persons; our personhood clearly matters and has inherent value. Therefore, if God is going to be a meaningful and transformative force in our lives, our hearts and imaginations must be engaged. God must have a "face" that is capable of seducing us. If we can't find a reason to love God, we won't follow God. But at the same time, when we personify God we face the very real danger of projecting our humanity onto God and reducing God to a self-serving idol, effectively stripping God of mystery. We end up making God into a progressive, a conservative, a Catholic, a Protestant, and so forth. But of course God transcends our politics, concepts, images, preferences, theologies, dogmas, and all other categories! God is absolutely transcendent: beyond everything, beyond the beyond. And yet, paradoxically, God is absolutely knowable. The Hindu master Paramahansa Yogananda tells us, "I say God is both personal and impersonal. He is the Absolute, beyond form, but He also makes Himself manifest in many ways. If there were no blue sky, no vast space, no beautiful scenery, no moon or twinkling stars in the heavens, we would never have suspected the existence of God at all. The wonders we behold in this universe suggest to us the immanence of God. He is visible everywhere, in everything He has created, and in the workings of His intelligence governing all of creation."[4]

Most importantly, Yogananda states, "God makes Himself known through the divinity in worthy instruments...purna avatars, liberated beings who are fully one with God; their return to earth is to fulfill a God-ordained mission... Without this intercession of God's love come to earth in the example, message, and guiding hand of His avatars, it would be scarcely possible for groping humanity to find the path into God's kingdom."[5] Simply, God becomes personal,

4. Paramahansa Yogananda, *The Divine Romance*, 2nd ed. (Los Angeles, CA: Self-Realization Fellowship, 2000), 377.
5. Paramahansa Yogananda, *The Second Coming of Christ* (Los Angeles, CA: Self-Realization Fellowship, 2004), 4.

knowable, and lovable in the person of a divine incarnation, a guru. For Kriyabans (and Christians) *"Christ is the visible image of the invisible God."*[6] Though Kriyabans also acknowledge Jesus as a divine incarnation, they also acknowledge other divine incarnations: Babaji is the *Great Avatar*; Lahiri Mahasaya, an incarnation of *Joy*; Sri Yukteswar, an incarnation of *Wisdom*; and Yogananda, an incarnation of *Love*. They are heavenly icons, revealing the very face of God to us. We will discuss the guru-disciple relationship fully in a later chapter.

Years ago, a spiritual mentor told me, "If you don't periodically feel as though you are lost or that the ground is shaking beneath your feet, you are probably out of touch with God." Therefore, whether we approach God through the mediation of an avatar or in the silence of absolute transcendence, the process is always the same: we must remain humble, teachable, and open to new and unheard of realizations. We must never think that we have reached the last realization, the final bliss, the deepest layer of silence, or the fullness of love. Why? Because the experience of God is inexhaustible!

Jesus the Christ: Christianity's Unique Gift

For Christians, Jesus is the very face of a personal God. What do the life and teachings of Jesus the Christ tell us about God? Most importantly, the story of Jesus reveals to us a humble God, a simple God, a

---

6. Colossians 1:15.

God of the people, and a God who suffers. Jesus was born not in a palace but in a stable, to pious but everyday parents of meager means. Given the fact that Joseph was not his biological father, we could technically say that Jesus was an illegitimate child. After Jesus' birth, his parents had to flee to Egypt in order to keep him out of harm's way, so Jesus was a refugee fleeing persecution. Rather than being fixated with the prestige of the Jerusalem Temple, Jesus spent most of his public ministry with everyday folk, especially those who were labeled as unclean – tax collectors, prostitutes, and Gentiles. His own people rejected him, and his intimate followers abandoned him in his darkest hour. And yes, he died a tortuous death at the hands of the Roman Empire.

I am not glorifying Jesus' suffering, but what I am emphasizing is that Jesus reveals to us a God that knows our human struggles, a God that embraces everyone, a God that weeps with us, a God that suffers with us, and a God that dies with us. The life of Jesus proclaims the truth that no matter how dark or painful our lives might be, God is with us. And if God is with us, so is the sustaining force of light and hope, as well as God's love and consolation. And just as God raised Jesus' decaying body to life, we too will be raised to a divinized and glorified existence. Jesus' life reveals the truth of all truths: that God's love is the most powerful force in all of creation!

So how do we begin to learn about the God of Jesus and the God of all of us? I prefer two contexts for the discussion of God. The first is the Hindu understanding of *Sat Chit Ananda*, which translates as *Existence,*

Consciousness, and Bliss, and the Christian understanding of the Holy Trinity, which is *Father, Son, and Holy Spirit.* My desire is to discuss the concept of God in a practical and understandable way which reveals the relational character of spirituality: God is always in relationship with us, and we are always in relationship with God – even though we are often unaware of it. But before we even begin, we must make peace with this truth: our logical and linear minds were made to understand creation, but not the creator! God is understood not with the mind but with the intuition and the heart. St. Augustine wisely said, "If you comprehend it, it is not God."[7]

God as Existence (Sat) and Father

Yes, God is a mystery, but a mystery that is endlessly knowable. When we approach God as *Sat,* we begin our study at its most abstract point. Be patient as we linger a bit in our discussion here, and remember that we are not called to intellectually *understand* this concept, but we are called to *experience* it and even to love it.

As a starting point, God is not a little man or woman sitting on a heavenly throne. God is not a demigod, that is, partly human and partly divine, not a being among beings, and not even a supreme being. God is the pure *Being-ness* of existence, the pure *Such-ness* of existence, the pure *Is-ness* of existence. The word *Sat* represents this concept. God is the one indivisible Re-

---

7. St. Augustine, *Tractates on the Gospel of John,* 38.10.

ality that is the source and sustainer of all things and all people, including you and me. At every moment of our lives we are resting in the great nest of God's being, and we are perpetually in relationship to God's Being-ness.

For this reason, God cannot be put under a microscope or empirically analyzed – because God is not a thing and does not have parts! God just *is*, without beginning or end, without moods, fluctuations, or changes. God's unchanging Being-ness becomes the ever-present foundation of our lives to the extent that we *experience* it. No matter what is happening around us or to us, we are always grounded in the unchanging reality of God. Death, therefore, is not the end of our existence but our transition into another dimension of our existence in God.

To make this concept of God a living reality in your life, think of God as the Root of all roots, the Source of all sources, and the Breath of all breaths. St. Paul tells us, "We live and move and have our being in God."[8] In a manner of speaking, God has donated our existence to us; our existence is a participation in God's existence. Therefore, we are never apart from God, but are perpetually *in* God, perpetually drawing our life from God, and perpetually sustained by God. Yes, God is the very ground of our being. We can't be where God is not! We don't *find* God. Rather, we *uncover the truth* that we are perpetually swimming in the ocean of God's presence. Yogananda wrote, "I am Thy dewdrop that floats on Thy shoreless sea."[9] Put

---

8. Acts 17:28.
9. Paramahansa Yogananda, *Whispers From Eternity* (Los Angeles, CA: Self-Realization Fellowship, 1986), 132.

another way, God is always hiding in plain sight: within you, within me, within everyone – as the Soul of all souls. Jesus tells us, "The Kingdom of God is within you."[10] Spirituality, then, is not about finding God, but about removing the scales from our eyes, so that we can learn once again to see God, to delight in God, to adore God – for to know God is to love God. With beautiful simplicity, Francis of Assisi tells us, "God is without beginning and without end, unchangeable, indivisible, indescribable, ineffable, incomprehensible, unfathomable, blessed, worthy of praise, glorious, exalted on high, sublime, most high, gentle, lovable, delectable, and totally desirable above all else forever."[11]

God as *Sat*, as Existence, corresponds to the *Father* of the Christian Trinity. The Trinity points us in the direction of relationship because we did not create ourselves; the source of our existence is not ourselves, but God. We are not a closed system; we exist perpetually in God and because of God. For this reason, Christians rightly speak of God as Father.

While the doctrine of the Trinity might seem heady or overly theological, it has great implications for the quality of our day-to-day lives. We are social creatures! We only thrive in the context of relationships. We exist in relationship to God's generosity as children of God's Being-ness. The Trinity implies that at the very heart and soul of God is the reality of relationship, of generosity and receptivity. More specifically, we uncover the mystery of who we are only in

---

10. Luke 17:21.
11. *365 St. Francis of Assisi*, trans. Murray Bodo (London: Fount, 1987), 204.

the context of the relationship between heaven and earth, angels and humans, guru and disciple, one to another, and extending to all of creation. Those who advance spiritually are able to be relational, to be part of a spiritual community or lineage. They are able to bear both the joys and the sufferings of relationships. In this spirit, every authentic spiritual master always creates a community of followers.

God as Pure Consciousness (Chit) and Son

Yes, God is pure unadulterated existence, but now we come to a personal question: is God conscious? Is God conscious of you and me? Is God conscious of the world? What mystics the world over tell us is that God is an infinite ocean of pure Consciousness – ever-awake, ever-present, ever-resplendent, ever-luminous – that envelops all that is. The word *Chit* represents this Consciousness. This means that God is entirely and equally conscious of everyone, including you and me. We are always in the very center of the Divine Mind; thus, every tear shed, every prayer whispered, every hope expressed is held in the Consciousness of God. Jesus tells us, "Even the hairs on your head are numbered."[12]

Continuing to question, we wonder, does God's Consciousness make a difference in the large and small details of our lives? Jesus tells us, "Not even a sparrow falls to the ground outside of your Father's care."[13]

---

12. Matthew 10:30.
13. Matthew 10:29.

Therefore, the Consciousness of God is the dynamic and organizing force within creation which guides every aspect of humankind's evolution, and this Consciousness responds to our sincere aspirations for healing, growth, and enlightenment. To the degree that we give ourselves over to the organizing force of God's Consciousness, we allow God's light to explicitly shape our destiny.

Furthermore, unlike a flame which flickers in the wind, God's Consciousness is always absolute, always complete, always full, always steady, and always the same. Our sins don't lessen it and our virtues don't add to it. Jesus explained the absolute steadiness of God's Consciousness when he said, "...so that you might be like your Father in heaven. He makes the sun rise on both the evil and the good, and he sends rain on the just and the unjust."[14]

Perhaps what is most incredible is the truth that our consciousness emerges from the Consciousness of God and is a participation in that very same Consciousness. Put another way, at the very center of human awareness is a spark of divine light emanating from God, giving light to our minds and spirits. Enlightenment is not some esoteric experience, but the simple process of allowing more and more of God's light, God's intelligence, to illumine our understanding – helping us to see as God sees.

I have had the privilege of being in the presence of a few individuals I consider to be saints. My experience of them has always included a sense of clearness,

---

14. Matthew 5:45.

alertness, a discernible luminosity, simplicity, an ever-present wakefulness, and a wide seeing-ness. Just being in their presence makes me more attentive, more alive, more understanding, more involved, and more open to new possibilities. These saints are not genetically different than you or me; they are just more available to the light of God's Consciousness. They mirror our own potential to consciously attune ourselves to the Divine Mind.

Chit, or Consciousness, relates to what Christians refer to as the *Son*, the second person of the Holy Trinity. Yogananda tells us that the "Christ Consciousness or Son is the conscious Presence of God's intelligent divine plan in creation."[15] In the silent and mysterious Being-ness of God are the seeds of all that we legitimately and wholesomely desire – potential manifestations of truth, beauty, and goodness. These seeds blossom fully in the Son – in Christ Consciousness.

Christians hold to be true, rightly so, that Jesus of Nazareth is the perfect embodiment of the Christ Consciousness, that is, the very incarnation of the Divine Mind. This truth is embodied in the prologue of John's Gospel: "In the beginning was the word. The word was with God and the Word was God. He was in the beginning with God. All things came to be through him, and without him nothing came to be... And the Word became flesh and made his dwelling among us."

It is important to point out, however, that the Son or the Christ Consciousness has manifested in and

---

15. Paramahansa Yogananda, *The Second Coming*, 13.

through more historical figures than Jesus, such as Krishna, Babaji, the Buddha, and Anandamayi Ma. This is not heresy, but a reality which reflects the generosity of the Godhead. Within the lineage of Kriya Yoga, we intuitively believe that our gurus embody and express the very same Christ Consciousness that Jesus embodied and expressed. Jesus said, "By their fruits you shall know them."[16] The fruits that these great masters manifested could only come from one source: the Son, the Logos, the Christ Consciousness, the organizing intelligence of God.[17]

Really, we all have the capacity to tap into the unlimited reservoir of Divine Intelligence – the Christ Consciousness – that percolates within us and within all of creation. Christians, for example, are not meant to merely worship Christ, but to manifest the very same consciousness that he manifested. We are meant to move through life's challenges, spiritual or mundane, guided by the very Mind of God. Lahiri Mahasaya tells us, "Attune yourself to the active inner Guidance; the Divine Voice has the answer to every dilemma of life. Though man's ingenuity for getting himself into trouble appears to be endless, the Infinite Succor is no less resourceful."[18]

Returning to the doctrine of the Holy Trinity, we realize again that the spiritual life is all about relation-

---

16. Matthew 7:16–20.
17. Not all legitimate spiritual paths equally reflect the Christ Consciousness, but they do reflect a level of the Christ Consciousness. In any given lifetime, people follow the path they need to follow in order to evolve. Having said this, what is clear is that the mystics of these different traditions are drinking from the same spring of Living Water. Truly, we are all brothers and sisters!
18. Paramahansa Yogananda, *Autobiography of a Yogi* (Los Angeles, CA: Self-Realization Fellowship, 2010), 285.

ship. Jesus the Christ, the Son, received all that the Father wanted to give him. Are we willing to attune ourselves to the Divine Mind; yes, to sit at the feet of a God-realized guru? Are we willing to be receptive and open and childlike? Are we willing to obey, to listen, to align our lives to the momentum of truth? The more we say *yes* to the forces of truth, beauty, and goodness, the more operative these forces become in our lives, and the more Christ-like we become.

God as Bliss (Ananda) and Holy Spirit

In discussing Bliss and the Holy Spirit, a story from my psychotherapy practice might be helpful. Many years ago, parents brought their 16-year-old son to see me because he was suffering from a low level form of depression. Though I tried for a number of sessions, I was unable to help him break free of his melancholy moods. Then it happened. He came to a session with a bounce in his step and a twinkle in his eye. When I asked him what was up, he replied, "I met Maria. I'm in love, and I am happy!" My young client was actually experiencing a subtle and partial manifestation of *Ananda*, God's Bliss.

Properly understood, Ananda is more than a passive form of joy. Ananda is the very heart of God! Ananda is what Christians refer to as the *Holy Spirit* or *Agape*, that is, Divine Love. As such, Ananda is an intelligent, purposeful, and dynamic Force. It is the nature of Ananda, of Love, to overflow and to generate life. You and I are the offspring of this overflow; we have been loved into existence and are directly sustained by the energy of Divine Love. We abide in this Love and this Love abides in us, or we would cease to exist.

The Spirit of Love that enlivened and illumined the consciousness of Jesus, Francis, and Yogananda is the same Spirit that is within all of us. Again, we ask ourselves a question like this: How open to the transforming energy of the Spirit do we want to be? How much light and joy are we willing to bear? Do we long to be wholly possessed by Love? The entire path of Kriya Yoga serves one ultimate purpose: to open us to Divine Love. The spiritual life is simply the ever-deepening process of living a divine life, of becoming one with the force of Love. Saint Bonaventure offers us a challenging but simple path to the realization of our ultimate destiny as he writes, "If you wish to know how these things may come about, ask for grace, not learning; desire, not understanding, the groaning of prayer, not diligence in reading; the Bridegroom, not the teacher; God, not man; darkness, not clarity; not light, but the fire that wholly inflames and carries one into God through transporting unctions and consuming affections. God Himself is this fire."[19]

A Meditation

Words are vibrations, and vibrations effect change. Meditating on sacred words purifies our awareness

---

19. St. Bonaventure, *The Journey of the Mind to God*, trans. Philotheus Boehner (Indianapolis, IN: Hackett Publishing Company, 1993), 39.

and opens us to God's transformative presence. When we meditate on *Sat Chit Ananda* we avail ourselves of the experience of God. The practice is very simple: Sit in a chair, with your head and neck aligned and your spine gently erect. To steady your breath, pause for a second or two after inhalation, and then release a steady, even exhalation. After breathing in this manner for five minutes, mentally add the mantra *Om* on inhalation, pause for a second or two, and mentally repeat *Sat Chit Ananda* on the exhalation. Do this for five minutes or so, and when there is peace or stillness, let it all go and just rest in God's presence.

God and Gender

At times, my mother would refer to God as the "little man upstairs." Believing her, I actually ventured into our attic in search of this little man. But alas, I found only dust and a very large spider. Most of us are sophisticated enough to know that God is not physically anything, yet alone a specific gender. Yet, God encompasses the mystery of what we know as feminine and masculine energies. After all, the book of Genesis tells us, "God created mankind in his own image, in the image of God he created them; male and female he created them."[20] We must, therefore, resist the modern tendency to neuter God and ourselves. We must celebrate the magic of God's energy in all of its manifested forms.

Of course, God in God's transcendence is beyond all

---

20. Genesis 1:27.

polarities, including masculine or feminine polarities. As such, God is the simple unity of all that is true, beautiful, and good. But just as a light passing through a prism fractures into different hues of color, God's perfect simplicity expresses itself in a multiplicity of forms as it enters into the prism of creation. Hence, both feminine and masculine archetypes are essential manifestations of Divinity in the context of creation. In point of fact, spirituality without feminine energy tends to be overly authoritative, excessively logical, and legalistic – establishing truth over and against love. Spirituality without masculine energy is overly subjective, passive, and vapid – setting up love over and against truth. Truth without love is not truth, and love without truth is not love. In short, we need God as both Father and Mother!

Divine Mother

Yogananda perfectly captures the grace of the Mother as he writes, "Our relationship with God should be one of unconditional love. More than in any other relationship we may rightfully and naturally demand a reply from Spirit in Its aspect as the Divine Mother. God is constrained to answer such an appeal; for the essence of a mother is love and forgiveness of her child, no matter how great a sinner he may be."[21]

All of the world's great spiritual teachers and gurus entered creation through a mother. What truth does

---

21. Paramahansa Yogananda, *How You Can Talk With God* (Los Angeles, CA: Self-Realization Fellowship, 1957), 9.

this fact reveal to us? God's grace enters the human family, and our lives, always through the Mother, through Her tenderness and loving presence. Therefore, devotion to the Divine Mother is not a pleasant option, but a necessity. Why? Because the spiritual life begins with grace and is consummated in grace. Yogananda tells us, "Devotees of all ages, approaching the Mother in a childlike spirit, testify that they find Her ever at play with them."[22]

The Divine Mother is not merely an impersonal archetype; Her consciousness becomes embodied in advanced souls, in avatars. In the Roman Catholic and Orthodox Christian traditions, Mary is referred to as the *Mother of God* and is sometimes described as the *Face of the Holy Spirit*. The Quran describes her as *She Who Has Never Sinned*. Mary's devotees are many, and her grace, which has flowed through her many apparitions, remains a powerful force in the lives of her followers and in the world. Before I go to bed each night I pray the rosary, using each bead to represent a person for whom I am praying. For me, the rosary is not only an effective way of praying for others, but also a way to draw closer to the heart of my spiritual mother.

In the Hindu tradition, Yogananda called Anandamayi Ma the *Joy-Permeated Mother*.[23] Though she was uneducated, scholars sought her wisdom; devotees, her grace. Many healings have been attributed to her, and even though she left the body in 1982, Anandamayi Ma continues to draw devotees from all

---

22. Paramahansa Yogananda, *Autobiography*, 72.
23. Ibid., 385.

corners of the globe. Truly, she personifies the love and light of the Divine Mother! I find her teachings to be expressions of pure truth and powerfully transformative.

Saint Francis of Assisi dedicated his religious order, the Order of Friars Minor, to Mary, the Blessed Mother. Yogananda dedicated his mission to the Divine Mother. Accordingly, we at The Assisi Institute have dedicated our entire mission to the care of the Divine Mother, and we honor both the Blessed Mother and Anandamayi Ma as our spiritual mothers.

God is Simple

I will close with quotes from my two favorite spiritual writers: Yogananda and the Christian mystic Valentin Tomberg. Their wisdom guides my life on a daily basis, and they have my loving devotion for all of eternity.

One day when Tomberg was four years old, he asked his mother, "Where is God? Is he in heaven? Does he float there? Or is he sitting? Where?"

His mother answered, "God is present everywhere: where the air is invisible and penetrates everything. Just as we live and breathe in the air, and it is thanks to the air that we live and breathe, so our souls live and breathe God and it is thanks to him that we live."

As Tomberg recounts that childhood memory, he writes, "The answer was so clear and convincing that, like a breath of fresh air, it blew away all conceptual problems and left behind certainty concerning God's invisible presence everywhere. This 'seed' thought later grew into the heights and depths and breadths, representing the primal seed from which there grew a many-branched tree of insight and faith during the subsequent decades of the author's life."[24]

And from my beloved Yogananda,

"God is love. His plan for creation is rooted only in love. Does not that simple thought, rather than erudite reasonings, offer solace to the human heart? Every saint who has penetrated to the core of Reality has testified that a divine universal plan exists and that it is beautiful and full of joy."[25]

I hope this chapter has prompted you to consider your own concepts about the mystery of God – and to realize that God is bigger than any concept we could ever imagine. So how could we ever lose touch with such an immanent, ever-present, ever-loving God? I invite you to accompany me onward for an exploration of "waking up."

---

24. Valentin Tomberg, *Lazarus Come Forth!* (Great Barrington, MA: Lindisfarne Books, 2006), 264 – 265.
25. Paramahansa Yogananda, *Autobiography*, 420.

2 WAKING UP

A Parable

Just after God finished creating earth, he called all of the beloved souls together and asked them this question: "How many of you love me enough to accept a mission on earth?" Most of the beloved souls raised their hands. God continued, "But before you commit, let me give you the details: you will have a physical body that is truly a marvelous creation, but it will also cause you to experience pain and eventually death." Some of the souls put their hands down. "You will have to work by the sweat of your brow, and you will be confronted with endless challenges. Worse yet, you will forget about me and our loving union." More souls put their hands down. "Finally, you will forget that you have forgotten!" After this explanation only the bravest of the souls continued to raise their hands. God asked, "Do you have any questions?"

Concerned, the bravest souls asked, "But will you still be with us? Must we forget you forever?"

God replied, "I love you! I will never stop loving you, and I will always be with you, helping you, but unseen. Eventually, you will know the pure joy of waking up and remembering our union. Your remembering will give me great joy! And then together, we will work to bring about the perfect marriage of heaven and earth."

The bravest souls cried, "Let it be done according to your word!"

Given the fact that you are reading these words, never doubt your courage or your love for God. You are one of the bravest souls.

Waking Up

St. Paul tells us, "We live and move and have our being in God."[26] A fundamental truth of the spiritual life is that it is not about perfecting the personality or winning God's favor. God's favor is always given or we would cease to exist! Everything is predicated on grace. Therefore, the spiritual life is not about struggling to find God, but it is about removing the clouds of ignorance that hide God from us.

A prayer by Saint Augustine says it all: "Thou hast made us for thyself, O Lord, and our hearts are rest-

26. Acts 17:28.

less until they find their rest in Thee."[27] The Divine
Spark within us cannot be extinguished! Propelled by
the faint memory of paradise, we pour ourselves into
our happiness projects. But given the fact that we are
asleep, our happiness projects necessarily miss the
mark. As a result, we suffer. Suffering is not necessarily bad; it is, potentially, the first step in the process
of waking up. Suffering's intensity has a way of break-
ing through our sleepy dross and disturbing our habitual patterns. The goal of the spiritual life is not
necessarily freedom from suffering, but wakefulness in
the service of truth, beauty, and goodness. Therefore,
we must never despise the gift of tears.

Tears are often a sign that our spirits are being
touched by heaven's angels. Jesus wept at the tomb of
his friend Lazarus. Francis of Assisi wept before the
cross of San Damiano. Yogananda wept as he prayed
to the Divine Mother to send him a God-realized
guru. Wakefulness does not make us less human, but
more human as it moves us from a hard heart to a
fleshy, tender heart. Many people enter psychotherapy
because they believe that their dissatisfaction with life
is due to a psychological maladjustment, when in reality their pain is often a sign that their spirits are being stirred into wakefulness. What they need is not
analysis, but a spiritual path.

So suffering can disturb our sleep, but by itself suffering can never fully wake us. Something else is needed.
Here, a concrete example might be helpful. In my
psychotherapy practice, I have assisted families in
providing interventions for family members who suf-

---

27. St. Augustine, *Confessions*, I.

fer from alcoholism. There are always three essential ingredients involved with a successful intervention: love, truth, and help. If families do not speak the truth in love and offer their loved ones hope for a better future in the form of treatment, alcoholics will typically choose to cling to their addiction because the reality of their painful unmanageability is just too great. Alcoholics must be given a way out of the addictive spiral. A power greater than themselves is needed.

The Grace of a Higher Power

Most of us spend a great deal of our lives in the middle of a civil war of sorts. We want to wake up, we want to uncover our true selves, and we want to experience union with God. But we resist facing the fundamental fear and shame that underlies the human condition because the pain appears to be unbearable. So we cling to our psychological defenses and live at the surface of our awareness while we simultaneously grasp for happiness in all the wrong places and endure even more suffering, thus reinforcing our ego-directed compulsiveness.

Trying to free ourselves from this interior hell is like a man sinking in quicksand who tries to save himself by pulling up on his ponytail; it just does not work! Something from the outside, a force from above, must break into our downward spiral.

What is this force? What is this lovingly powerful force field which is capable of elevating us above and beyond the gravitational pull of our fear, shame, and maladaptive coping strategies? Some might call it Grace; others, Higher Power. Some feel comfortable with names like Spirit or The Absolute. I call it God. Regardless of what we call it, this very real transcendental force is the only foundation for a truly liberated life.

As a young man, I struggled to find peace. I knew that the solution was to be more deeply rooted in God, but I did not know how to consistently attune myself to the Divine Presence. The breakthrough came when a friend gave me a copy of Yogananda's *Autobiography of a Yogi*. It was as if my eyes were suddenly opened! I saw the hand of God pulling me out of the muck and mire of my self-induced misery. I was given a tried and true map to freedom in the form of a spiritual path that spoke to every aspect of my humanity, and I was initiated into an ever-deepening relationship with the God of wisdom and love.

My experience, which is not unique, underscores a universal truth: we don't stir ourselves into wakefulness. Rather, we respond to grace, to the stirrings of the Holy Spirit. Otherwise, the combination of our own inertia and the gravity of the human condition is too great to overcome. God's grace always comes first!

On the Way to Emmaus

A story in the Gospel of Luke perfectly captures the

truth about Divine Grace.[28] Two of Jesus' disciples were on the road to a town called Emmaus, which historians believe was little more than a Roman garrison. They were fleeing Jerusalem because Jesus had just been crucified, and they feared for their own lives. The symbolism is powerful: Jerusalem represents God's presence. The disciples' fear drove them away from the flow of grace and toward a worldly source of safety and security. Like all of us, they were traveling in the wrong direction.

While they walked toward Emmaus, a stranger joined them. In reality, the stranger was the risen Christ, but they didn't recognize him, just as God and guru are often in our midst, inspiring us, unrecognized. Notice that it was God who made the first move! Jesus did not come to walk with them because they were spiritually liberated, but precisely because they were lost. Likewise, God does not love us because we are good, but because God is good. The God who sent us here will not abandon us. No one is asleep forever!

While the two disciples talked with the unrecognized Jesus, they felt their "hearts burning within them."[29] Authentic spirituality always moves us to a greater level of wakefulness, to an open, transparent, and warm heart, and to the cultivation of presence, understanding, and expanded awareness.

As the story continues, Jesus bid the disciples goodbye, but they pleaded with him to remain with them, and he agreed to do so. The disciples' asking Jesus to

---

28. Luke 24:13–35.
29. Luke 24:32.

stay indicates something essential to the spiritual life: their willingness to cooperate with grace. The miracle of waking up is always the fruit of two wills, one divine and the other human. Spiritual realization, or wakefulness, begins with God's grace. But in order for the liberation loop to be completed, we must freely choose to say yes and to exercise our God-given freedom.

To the degree that we are asleep, we are not free. We are driven by raw instinct, psychological conditioning, and unconscious impulses – the forces of karma. The seed of freedom might percolate within us as a vague intuition, but we continue to be overshadowed by drives we neither see nor understand. Therefore, part and parcel of the waking up process is the rediscovery of our capacity for freedom.

After Jesus agreed to remain with the disciples, he "broke bread"[30] with them. In other words, he initiated them into a spiritual practice. Again, the disciples had to exercise their newly reawakened freedom in order to receive what Jesus wanted to give them. Every great spiritual master initiates his or her disciples into a practice whereby they can deepen their conscious contact with God. This very same process of initiation is an essential aspect of Kriya Yoga. Yogananda initiates disciples into the process of daily meditation, but meditation is not necessary for our physical survival, unlike eating and sleeping. By responding positively to the grace-filled invitation to meditate, the disciples of Yogananda are choosing to wake up, to avail themselves of grace, and to choose

---

30. Luke 24:30.

the path of love.

Christian mystic Valentin Tomberg writes, "Meditation arises from free initiative, from one's full consciousness. What happens, then, when One gives oneself over to meditation? A stream flows upward to the higher 'I' and to the angel (and guru), and a connection arises – consciousness is linked with superconsciousness. From superconsciousness a stream of light begins to flow downward and it strengthens the downward current that flows into the subconscious. This stream of light that has become highly conscious illumines now the subconscious, purifying it."[31]

What was the fruit of the disciples' choice to cooperate with this stranger's initiation rite? They recognized him as the resurrected Christ, and their joy was complete. Furthermore, they turned away from Emmaus and headed back to Jerusalem – symbolically, the focal point for spiritual realization. As we consciously choose to meditate and follow the path of Kriya Yoga, we grow increasingly more awake. We begin to realize our true nature as souls fashioned in the Divine Image, and we start to see God's presence percolating within all of creation, including ourselves. Thus, our life of joy begins!

What Happens When We Wake Up?

As we continue to consider the concept of wakeful-

---

31. Valentin Tomberg, *Inner Development* (Great Barrington, MA: Anthroposophic Press, 1992), 39.

ness, we might wonder exactly what it is that wakes up within us. According to Yogananda and the witness of the Judeo-Christian Scriptures, human beings are more than rational animals; we are God's very image! The interchangeable terms Yogananda uses to describe the Divine Image are Self and soul. He tells us, "Self is capitalized to denote the soul, man's true identity, in contradistinction to the ego or pseudosoul, the lower self with which man temporarily identifies through ignorance of his real nature."[32] Practically speaking, this implies that we were created to live as gods, not apart from God, but in God and with God! In our state of forgetfulness, however, we have lost contact with our true center, the Self, the soul. Therefore, we are perpetually restless, trying to find happiness in created things rather than finding rest in the Creator. It is the memory of who we are, the memory of home, and the memory of God that propels us forward. Saint Augustine tells us, "God is more I than I myself am."[33]

What does waking up look like? Is it entirely personal, or is there a universal experience or pattern? Because what we ultimately wake up to is God's presence, which is paradoxically personal yet transpersonal, the essential map is consistent among sincere seekers.

Most often, the waking up process begins with a sense of peace. In this context, peace is neither the absence of conflict nor a pleasant mood. Rather, peace is a manifestation of God's Being-ness. It flows from an

---

32. Paramahansa Yogananda, *The Second Coming*, 1591.
33. St. Augustine, *Confessions*, III.

unending stillness, silence, or spaciousness. This peace is not a dull or vegetative state of mind, but a living and dynamic peace. This peace silences the torturous activity of the ego.

Compassion is another element of the waking up process. Compassion is a kind of loving kindness which allows us to be gentle, loving, and accepting with ourselves and others. Compassion allows us to accept the unacceptable. It liberates us to be present to our joy and our pain as well as to our virtues and our flaws, which is absolutely necessary for spiritual growth. What opens us to the experience of compassion, I believe, is the intuition that God is infinitely compassionate toward us because God's very nature is compassion.

As we wake up, we also become more joyful. Both pleasure and happiness are based on the fulfillment of wishes and desires. By contrast, joy or bliss is innate to the soul, to God. Therefore, joy is unconditional! Joy arises effortlessly whenever we are touching our own souls or are conscious of the presence of God. Spiritual teacher A.H. Almaas gives us a wonderful description of the experience of joy: "The state of joy is that of lightness, delight, enjoyment, and sweetness. One becomes a radiance, a playfulness, a carefree presence. One delights in reality. One sees life as a light and playful adventure. Every moment is a source of singular joy, for it is the very presence of the Truth. One realizes that joy is the radiance of love, which is the breath of Truth."[34]

Of course, as we wake up we become more loving. Love has both a feminine and a masculine component. The feminine aspect of love is a joyful or blissful appreciation of the other person. Underlying this appreciation is the capacity to see beyond the personality or the ego and to see the radiance of the true Self. The masculine side of love is the willingness to serve the highest good of the other, whether or not it is easy. Love is the very Breath of God released into creation. It is the force that sustains and evolves us. Love brings us into union with God, each other, and our own souls. Love is the ultimate sign that determines the legitimacy of our spiritual experiences. Jesus said, "Everyone will know you are my disciples by your love for one another."[35]

No description of the waking up process would be complete without mentioning the re-emergence of moral memory. In traditional terms, moral memory is the equivalent of conscience. As we wake up, we begin to remember that creation is guided by an intelligent, purposeful, moral force. When we are moving in the wrong direction, we sense a lack of intuitive rightness and the presence of an interior discomfort. When we are in harmony with the intentions of God or the moral order, we sense an emerging peace, joy, and strength, even if the direction we are taking is challenging. Our conscience aligns us with God's

34. A.H. Almaas, *The Pearl Beyond Price* (Boston, MA: Shambala, 2001), 313. Almaas is a spiritual teacher whose theory of spiritual development, known as the Diamond Approach, is informed by modern psychology. Almaas is like a Jnana yogi, that is, one who follows the path of wisdom and discrimination.
35. John:13:35.

truth, with Reality. This alignment becomes a supportive, grounding, and strengthening energy in our lives. We become strong because God is strong!

Spiritual Intensity

Think about life's most meaningful moments, both happy and sad: weddings, the birth of a child, or graduations; and losses, illnesses, or death. In such moments, our human awareness is intensified. Our feelings are stronger, our perceptions are heightened, our insights are more penetrating, we are more present to what is happening in the moment, and our capacity to love deepens. In this context, intensity is not inner tension, emotional intoxication, or psychological conflict, but an opening to dimensions of life that are typically outside of our consciousness. The more we open ourselves to spiritual intensity, the more alive, joyful, and intuitively intelligent we become.

Spiritual growth is synonymous with the intensification of our conscious awareness of life, most especially to the Divine Life percolating within ordinary, day-to-day events. I remember such a moment of intensity on the morning of my grandson Elijah's baptism. I woke up that morning with a sense of lively anticipation. Love bubbled up within me and a palpable sense of joy filled me. When Vicki and I arrived at the church, we both felt a sense of energy, grace, and spiritual presence. During both the Gospel reading and the baptism, my heart opened so wide that I went into a level of ecstasy, so much so that I had to fight back tears of pure bliss. Heavenly light seemed to be radiating from everyone and everything.

Of course, the intensity of that moment did not last. However, the experience left me with some lingering questions: Am I willing to be that intensely awake and aware in my everyday life? Am I willing to be that engaged in all of the affairs of my life? Am I willing to have my intuitive eye opened at all times? I don't mean to imply that the spiritual life should be a constant euphoric high. Rather, our spiritual evolution is literally an intensification of our capacity to be fully involved in life, to be open to new dimensions of reality, and to be fully present to God's presence in any and all circumstances – regardless if those circumstances are mundane or extraordinary, pleasant or painful, straightforward or mysterious.

As we progress on the spiritual path, the same essential question accompanies us: how intensely awake and alive do we want to be? This question is particularly poignant when we remember that our lives are a participation in the one Divine Life. Properly understood, conscious aliveness is an unending excursion into God-realization! Healthy spirituality is not about saving our souls, but about living a life which is magnificent, exquisite, and rich in meaning and purpose. In the next chapter, we will explore the various pathways that such a life can take. Stay tuned!

3 THE DESTINATION AND THE PATHWAY

The Destination and the Pathway Chapter

We humans are innately dissatisfied creatures. We always seem to want better, best, and bigger than the best. We are constantly trying to leap beyond ourselves. Surprisingly, this dissatisfaction is not a flaw, but a blessing. Why? Within the depths of our souls is the memory of paradise, of union with God. We have been created for God, for the highest truth, the highest beauty, and the highest good! Nothing short of the Eternal, the Infinite, and the Absolute will ever satisfy the hunger of our hearts. All of our addictions, compulsions, and out of control ambitions are, in reality, a misdirected search for God. Thank God for the gurus and saints who have found their way to God and left behind their lives and teachings to show us the ways to transcend ourselves.

While growing up in a very Catholic world, I was fascinated with stories of the saints, and I remain so to this very day. Their hunger to leap beyond themselves, their drive to transcend narrow self-interest, and their choice to live for something greater than themselves – for God, for others, for love – completely captivates me. Examples abound: Anthony of Egypt lived for over fifty-years as a desert hermit in his search for God. Hildegard of Bingen gave every fiber of her being to God by founding monasteries, writing theological, medicinal, and botanical texts, composing music, and authoring and performing plays. Francis of Assisi left behind a life of comfort, wealth, and ease, choosing instead to embrace radical poverty in the service of God. Joan of Arc, a 15th century visionary who in obedience to God helped to lead the French army to victory, gave her life to God in martyrdom. Mother Teresa gave up a relatively easy life teaching girls of wealthy families to serve the poorest of the poor.

As I began to study the lives of saints from the Kriya Yoga tradition, I was pleased to see the very same patterns that I so admired in the Catholic saints. Lahiri Mahasaya made a profound commitment to his meditative practice while selflessly raising a family, teaching Kriya Yoga, and fulfilling his societal duties. Paramahansa Yogananda embraced the life of a renunciate, founded a school for children, and willingly left it all when he moved to the United States at the behest of his guru. Daya Mata chose to become a disciple of Yogananda at the age of 17 and spent the rest of her life in the service of his mission. These saints point the way to our own leap into Divinity. They are our evolutionary brothers and sisters who show what is possible for all of us! The details may differ according to cultural nuances, but the destination is always the same.

So what does Kriya Yoga have to offer spiritual seekers? As a beginning point, I want to make it clear that Kriya Yoga is not a religion. The word *yoga* means union, and *kriya* refers to action. Kriya Yoga, therefore, refers to *actions that bring us into union with God*. The experience of union has ever deepening layers, beginning with Self-realization, expanding into Christ Consciousness, and eventually flowing into unadulterated God-Union. In a later chapter, I will discuss both the lifestyle and the process of interior transformation that lead to these levels of spiritual realization. For now, let us begin at the journey's end – the destination – and see where Kriya Yoga can take us.

Self-realization

Francis of Assisi once spent an entire night praying, "Who are you, O God, and who am I?"[36] One of the greatest temptations that we all face is the temptation to live from our surface or false self – from the personality. Life lived on the level of the false self is characterized by a sense of separation, anxiety, and inadequacy. This is not who we are or how God intended us to live! We are meant to live from the *Di-*

---

36. Richard Rohr's Daily Meditations, Jan 3 2016, https://cac.org/what-you-seek-is-what-you-are-2016-01-03/

vine Image, the *Self*, or the *soul*.

The Self is who we are in God and who God is in us. Simply put, we are part and parcel of God, and our identity is inseparable from God's identity. Our DNA is divine! Yogananda writes, "Self-realization is knowing – in body, mind, and soul – that we are one with the omnipresence of God; that we do not have to pray that it comes to us, that we are not merely near it at all times, but that God's omnipresence is our omnipresence; that we are just as much a part of Him now as we will ever be. All we have to do is improve our knowing."[37]

As we let go of our identification with the personality or the egoic self, we might experience a bit of anxiety because we have been so attached to our stories, compulsions, and survival strategies. But to the degree that we let go into our own depths, we experience the capacity to stand back and witness the mind's machinations. We experience peace, and we experience a sense of connectedness to something greater than ourselves. We know an interior completeness. We intuitively know that our lives are a part of a great and mysterious unfolding and that our very nature is blissful love. The Self cannot ultimately be defined or analyzed, no more than God can be defined or analyzed. However, we intuitively recognize the Self from within, and it increasingly draws our attention, absorption, and surrender.

---

37. Paramahansa Yogananda, *The Second Coming*, xxi – xxii.

Christ Consciousness

As wonderful as Self-realization is, by no means is it the last frontier of spiritual realization. Yogananda tells us that the next step is Christ Consciousness. Christ Consciousness is predicated upon a fundamental truth: the very intelligence of God resides in every particle of creation, not as a passive presence, but as a divinely loving and organizing force. Clearly, there is an intelligence functioning within creation that is prior to and larger than human intelligence. In fact, our intelligence is but a participation in this great, immeasurable intelligence. For example, every minute 300 million cells die in the human body, and every minute 300 million new cells come into being, knowing exactly what their job is in the human organism, with no conscious guidance from you or me. This is the Christ Consciousness, the intelligence of God! And the very same Christ Consciousness that is functioning within me is also functioning in you, in everyone, and in all of creation. The immeasurable gift of being a human being is that we can become conscious of and cooperate with this universal intelligence. Yogananda tells us, "A true Christian – a Christ-one – is one who frees his soul from the consciousness of the body and unites it with the Christ Intelligence pervading all of creation."[38]

Because we are all connected in and through the Christ Consciousness, we feel the first blush of it in compassion, an experiential sense of communion with others, and a willingness to feel their pain and joy. Regardless of differences in ethnicity, religion, gen-

---

38. Ibid., 27.

der, or sexual orientation, we are one humanity, one race, and one people. Yogananda writes, "A Christlike person loves all beings and actually feels every portion of the earth and vibratory space as the living cells of his own body."[39] Disciples of the great guru Lahiri Mahasaya witnessed his experience of Christ Consciousness one day when he was teaching. He suddenly gasped and cried out, "I am drowning in the bodies of many souls off the coast of Japan!"[40] Not coincidentally, the next day his disciples learned from a cable newspaper that a number of people had died when their ship sank off the coast of Japan.

Still deeper, the more surrendered we are to Christ Consciousness, the more the forces of creation align behind us, supporting all of our noble endeavors because we are one with the mind of God. Given the fact that we are working with and for God, creation works with and for us. Lahiri Mahasaya refers to this spiritual principle as he says, "When the self is in communion with a higher power, Nature automatically obeys, without stress or strain, the will of man."[41] Christ Consciousness unfolds to the degree that we are able to loosen the boundaries around our sense of self, to allow our psychological defenses to fall away, and to be willing to become vulnerable to beauty and goodness. In a state of Christ Consciousness, we choose to look upon creation with soft eyes. Christ Consciousness is the readiness to marry our understanding to truth and our hearts to love, so much so that we eventually become actual embodiments of truth and love.

---

39. Ibid., 131.
40. Paramahansa Yogananda, *Autobiography*, 285.
41. Ibid., 290.

Francis of Assisi captures the essence, beauty, and unitive nature of Christ Consciousness in his *Canticle of the Creatures*:

> Most High, all-powerful, all-good Lord, all praise is Yours, all glory, all honor, and all blessings. To you alone, Most High, do they belong, and no mortal lips are worthy to pronounce Your Name.
>
> Praised be You, my Lord, with all Your creatures, especially Sir Brother Sun, who is the day through whom You give us light. And he is beautiful and radiant with great splendor. Of You Most High, he bears the likeness.
>
> Praised be You, my Lord, through Sister Moon and the stars. In the heavens you have made them bright, precious, and fair.
>
> Praised be You, my Lord, through Brothers Wind and Air, and fair and stormy, all weather's moods, by which You cherish all that You have made.
>
> Praised be You, my Lord, through Sister Water, so useful, humble, precious, and pure.
> Praised be You, my Lord, through Brother Fire, through whom You light the night. He is beautiful and playful and robust and strong.
>
> Praised be You, my Lord, through our Sister, Mother Earth, who sustains and governs us, producing varied fruits with colored flowers and herbs.

Praise be You, my Lord, through those who grant pardon for love of You and bear sickness and trial. Blessed are those who endure in peace: By You, Most High, they will be crowned.

Praised be You, my Lord, through Sister Death, from whom no one living can escape. Woe to those who die in mortal sin! Blessed are they She finds doing Your Will; the second death can do them no harm.

Praise and bless my Lord and give Him thanks and serve Him with great humility.

God-realization: Cosmic Consciousness

Yogananda tells us, "The persevering devotee advances to the realization that God is Spirit, the Unmanifested Absolute."[42] This is to say that God is within creation, but also transcends creation. Saint Bonaventure writes, "God is in all things, but not enclosed."[43] If Christ Consciousness is the experience of God *within* creation, God-realization or Cosmic Consciousness is the experience of God *beyond* creation as pure existence (*Sat*), pure consciousness (*Chit*), and pure bliss (*Ananda*). Therefore, we do not experience God as an object, as a demigod, or even as a supreme being, but as unqualified Being-ness, as depthless Consciousness, and as unbounded Bliss.

---

42. Paramahansa Yogananda, *The Second Coming*, 311.
43. Richard Rohr's Daily Meditations, Nov 13, 2014 (This text is no longer available online, but in the book *A Spring Within Us*. See store.cac.org/A-Spring-Within-Us-A-Book-of-Daily-Meditations_p_427.html).

The imaginary line between God and us disappears in the experience of God-realization. Although the experience of God-realization is beyond words, it can be said to be the very essence of freedom, simplicity, and oneness. It is the unalloyed such-ness of God, the very essence of God's God-ness. It is not you or me being conscious of God, but just simple, unbounded God consciousness.

God-realization does not permit us to escape from life, but actually energizes us in all of our endeavors. Why? Because all of creation arises from God's Being-ness, just as a wave emerges from the ocean. And the more conscious we become of God's Being-ness, the more creatively dynamic we become. Think of how Francis of Assisi rebuilt the Catholic Church in the 12th century, how Yogananda came to this country with nothing and established a spiritual movement that continues to thrive years beyond his death, and how Mother Teresa began her religious order with no assets, yet managed to feed countless numbers of starving people. These spiritual giants were all grounded in the consciousness of God's simple Being-ness.

Pathways to God Realization:

What is the process that leads us to these ever-deepening layers of realization? Within the tradition of Kriya Yoga, realization unfolds according to four different but complimentary pathways: Raja Yoga, Bhakti Yoga, Jnana Yoga, and Karma Yoga. Each of these pathways provides a foundation for Kriya Yoga,

and each builds on our humanness: Raja, on energy;
Bhakti, on devotion; Jnana, on the mind, and Karma,
on the body. In actuality, these four pathways are
found in all of the world's spiritual traditions, though
they are named differently. Yes, God is one, and so is
the journey to God-realization! However these pathways are described or named, they have one powerful
underlying purpose: they work to expand us beyond
the false self, beyond the personality, beyond self-
absorption, and into greater and greater levels of
unity with our own souls, the souls of our fellow humans, the soul of creation, and God's own soul – and
all without ever diminishing our individuality. Put
another way, at the deepest level of our being, in the
depths of our souls, we love God and God's creation
because God is love, and we are God's very image.
Therefore, these pathways reveal to us the reality of
our oneness in God. Sincere devotees will display aspects of all four of these yogic pathways over time.

Raja Yoga: The Path of Meditation

Although Kriya Yoga incorporates all of the yogic
traditions, it is grounded in Raja Yoga, the "Royal
Path" to God-realization. Raja Yoga is the practice of
meditation and contemplation. *The goal of meditation
in the Kriya tradition is not the reduction of stress or en-
hanced health, as laudable as these might be, but union
with God.* Jesus says, "The kingdom of God is within
you."[44] Raja Yoga helps us to make Jesus' statement a
living reality. Lahiri Mahasaya sums up Raja Yoga in

---

44. Luke 17:21.

this way: "Withdrawing the mind from worldly matters, if one turns it inwards he will rediscover the hidden treasure inside."[45]

Human beings are comprised of body, emotion, mind, and energy. Raja Yoga helps us to consciously experience God's interior kingdom by collecting, intensifying, and directing our internal energy toward our higher chakras. The upward flow of our energy enlivens our chakras, heightens our spiritual awareness, and helps us to transcend the egoic mind, effectively preparing us for God-realization. Ultimately, the Kriya Yogi becomes a master of energy, of prana. Raja Yoga brings us to the conscious realization of God's indescribable presence within us by emptying us of ourselves, our attachments, and our preoccupation with our self-image. We can visit holy places, read the best of spiritual writings, and attend retreats – all of which are great blessings – but only deep meditation ultimately brings us home to God. Lahiri Mahasaya tells us, "The very touch of the master can elevate a sincere disciple to an advanced stage, but only his unceasing practice combined with love, faith, and devotion will lead him to God-realization."[46]

Richard Rohr captures the essence of Raja Yoga in this way: "The false self that you think you are or need to be is just an idea in your head. During quiet prayer, little by little, you become more naked and more vulnerable. It's like love-making. You slowly disrobe and become mirrored perfectly in the safety and gentleness of God's intimate presence. In prayer,

---

45. Paramahamsa Prajnanananda, *Lahiri Mahasaya: Fountainhead of Kriya Yoga* (Vienna, Austria: Prajna Publication, 2009), 99.
46. Ibid., 99.

you are allowing God to love you and to complete the circuit of love, which is the way all electricity must work – in a circuit. God sees the Christ in you and cannot *not* love you. That part of you – your True Self – has always loved God and has always said yes to God. Contemplative prayer is recognizing yourself in God and letting God recognize God's very Self in you. Now the circuit is complete, and the power called grace can flow freely."[47]

Though all the world sees Francis of Assisi as a servant of the poor and a friend to all of creation, we may not often realize that he spent half of his time in prayer, meditation, and solitude – which grounded him in the spirit of Raja Yoga. His experience of union with God energized him for his life of service to the world. Both Gandhi and Mother Teresa changed the world – not merely by the force of their personalities, but by the fact that their lives were steeped in prayer and meditation. The same was true of Dorothy Day.

Bhakti Yoga: The Path of Devotion

Jesus was once asked to name the greatest of all the commandments. In our time, we might ask him to explain the true meaning of religion and spirituality. Jesus said, "Thou shalt love the Lord thy God with all thy heart, and with all thy soul, and with all thy mind. This is the first and greatest commandment.

47. Richard Rohr's Daily Meditations, August 10, 2017, https://cac.org/completing-divine-circuit-2017-08-10/

And the second is like unto it, Thou shalt love thy neighbor as thyself. On these hang all the law and the prophets."[48] When Krishna was asked a similar question, he answered, "Those who adoringly pursue this undying religion (dharma) as heretofore declared, saturated with devotion, supremely engrossed in Me – such devotees are extremely dear to Me."[49]

Bhakti Yoga is the path of devotion, of all-surrendering love as the means for experiencing union with God. Bhakti takes negative or neutral emotions and brings them into the heart, where they become permeated with love. This makes our emotions, and us, sweet and pleasant. When people are in love, they are happy, open, and generous. They become better people. Bhakti Yoga takes the ordinary love affair and literally turns it into something extraordinary, a divine love affair. Yet, there is an inherent danger to the path of devotion. If we have not been purified, there is always a chance that we might fall in love with falling in love, using devotion masquerading as love to serve our own selfish needs. A person who becomes overly attached to the pleasant consolations of spirituality without ever becoming more loving or selfless shows us Bhakti Yoga gone wrong. For this reason, the ultimate expression of devotion, love, and surrender is expressed in the prayer, "Thy will be done," or "As you wish." Bhakti is the willingness to sacrifice self in the service of something greater than self. For example, Francis fell in love with Jesus when he heard Jesus say from the cross, "Francis, can't you see my church is crumbling? Go and rebuild it." The

---

48. Matthew 22:36–40.
49. Paramhansa Yogananda, *The Bhagavad Gita*, 857.

proof of Francis' love was his obedience. He literally went about repairing abandoned churches at great cost to himself: his father disowned him, he was temporarily imprisoned, and people accused him of madness. And yet, because he was motivated by love, he endured everything with great joy. His joy attracted more and more followers, and he ended up revitalizing the entire Catholic Church.

Finally, Bhakti Yoga imparts a kind of intuitive intelligence that is greater than the capacities of the intellect. The intellect can scrutinize certain aspects of God, but only love gives us the experience of God. The Bhakti yogi simply embraces and experiences the truth, whether or not it makes sense to the intellect. He or she lives life with childlike simplicity, concerned only with pleasing the Beloved. Therese of Liseux, the Little Flower, showed us the path of Bhakti. We describe her path as the *Little Way*, the loving surrender to God in all circumstances.

Jnana Yoga: The Path of Wisdom

Jnana Yoga is the path of wisdom, discernment, and razor sharp discrimination. It is neither the denial nor the glorification of human intelligence. Rather, Jnana Yoga is the marriage of our intelligence to a moral intelligence, the marriage of our understanding to a transcendental understanding, and the marriage of our mind to the Divine Mind. It is the intellect bowing to the light of intuition. Jnana Yoga is the choice to obey our inspired conscience, over and against the impulsive nature of the false self. Clearly, Jnana Yoga weans us from the egoic tendency to rationalize our choices by attuning us to our soul's promptings, to the voice of God.

To understand the depth and power of Jnana Yoga, we must understand the source of its wisdom. This source is not academic knowledge, logic, or analysis, but what Christians refer to as the *Logos* and yogis call the *Supermind.* It is the very intelligence of the Divine as a light-force leaning into human consciousness. To the degree that we open to this light-force, it transforms our being and our consciousness and makes right the conditions of our lives. We know we are being guided by wisdom because we experience clarity, peace, strength, and an intense alertness. When we are moving away from wisdom, our conscience notifies us under the guise of discomfort, confusion, and agitation.

Francis also followed the path of Jnana Yoga. He did not study philosophy, theology, or psychology, but he meditated on the words of scripture. He practiced silence so that he could hear the Spirit whispering to him. He always sought the highest good in all situations by nurturing a beginner's mind, being faithful to the vows he had taken, and giving others permission to correct him. Jnana Yoga freed him from the shackles of his false self, thereby liberating him to live from his true Self, his God-Self. Gandhi showed the wisdom of a Jnana Yogi when he courageously called off a huge demonstration after it had started because he realized that he had not been listening to his conscience.

What does Jnana Yoga mean for us as householders living in the world? To begin with, our prayer and meditative silence is the precondition for wise and inspired discrimination, for hearing the voice of God. There are also basic questions that we continually ask ourselves as we seek right discernment: do I want what I want or what God wants? Is this action going to bring me closer to God or not? Is it helping or hurting others? Is my conscience at peace with this choice? Is what I am proposing to do in alignment with the teachings of Kriya Yoga, the Ten Commandments, or Jesus' Beatitudes? Am I endeavoring to surrender to God's will?

Karma Yoga: The Path of Service

The last foundation stone of Kriya Yoga is Karma Yoga, defined as service to God, to guru, and to others. The Karma yogi is the mother getting up in the middle the night to feed her newborn baby. It is the father going to work day after day to a job that is less than rewarding so that he can care for his family. It is those who spend periodic nights serving in a homeless shelter. It is sharing our time, talent, and treasure in support of the guru's mission. It is allowing our bodies and lives to be used as instruments of God's love. Karma Yoga makes our spirituality real, human, and practical. Jesus said, "All men will know you are my disciples by your love for one another."[50] It is important to note that while Francis of Assisi was rebuilding churches, he and his early followers lived

---

50. John 13:35.

among lepers, caring for their needs and providing food and fellowship. In his hands-on service Francis embodied the love of God for his suffering brothers and sisters, making him a true Karma yogi.

It is important to remember that Karma Yoga is rooted in the spirit of nonattachment. What does this mean? It means that we give without any expectation of receiving, and that we are not attached to the outcome of our service. To the degree that we want things to turn out a certain way or that we get upset when the outcome is different than our expectations, the egoic self, not love, is still motivating us. Dr. Martin Luther King, Jr. lovingly embodied the spirit of Karma Yoga. He dedicated his life to non-violent resistance, the eradication of racism, and the alleviation of suffering. Yet, he knew that the movement he led was not about his agenda, but God's agenda. Listen to the words he spoke the night before he was assassinated: "Like anybody, I would like to live a long life. Longevity has its place. But I'm not concerned about that now. I just want to do God's will. And He's allowed me to go up to the mountain. And I've looked over, and I've seen the Promised Land. I may not get there with you. But I want you to know tonight, that we, as a people, will get to the Promised Land."[51]

Our service has to be selfless, or else it is not true Karma Yoga. Karma Yoga can be challenging. We can feel disappointed when people make wrong decisions which hurt themselves or others, but we are not overwhelmed by sadness, and we do not regret giving of

---

51. Dr. King's speeches are easily accessible in books and online.

ourselves. We surrender the fruit of our action, the results, to God. This surrender is essential, especially in our present political climate. Many well-meaning people are engaged in worthwhile causes, trying to make a positive difference. But when their efforts do not produce the hoped for outcome, two things tend to happen: burn out and a militant anger, both of which do nothing but cause more suffering. Karma Yoga reminds us again and again that God is in charge of all outcomes! Mother Teresa once said, "God does not want us to be necessarily successful, just faithful."[52]

Which path to follow?

How do we know which path of yoga to follow? God gives unique gifts to each person, so each person will express his or her love for God a bit differently. Those who are more devotionally oriented will choose the path of Bhakti; those who have a keen, discriminating intelligence will naturally be drawn to Jnana Yoga, and those who are action oriented will choose the path of Karma Yoga. Those who are more intuitive or introverted will gravitate toward Raja Yoga. Maturing devotees will integrate aspects of all of these pathways to greater or lesser degrees.

We cannot help but aspire to the highest happiness, the highest good, the highest beauty, and the highest truth. We don't have to be ashamed of our aspira-

52. Christie Arnold, *A Lesson from Mother Teresa*, thepapist.org/a-lesson-from-mother-teresa/

tions. They come from God, and God has given us the means to fulfill them. We have the God-given potential to experience all that God experiences. It is not our cleverness that will fulfill our deepest longings, but our loving surrender to God – in and through the practices of Raja Yoga, Bhakti Yoga, Jnana Yoga, and Karma Yoga. Our loving relationship with the guru will allow our practices to grow in exactly the right ways and at the right times. And to the relationship with guru we turn next.

4 THE GURU

Interconnectedness and Initiation

The guru-disciple relationship is a beautifully spiritual reflection of the interconnectedness of all life. Every time we exhale, for example, the trees inhale our breath. And every time the trees exhale, we inhale the oxygen they breathe into the environment. We do not exist as independent islands, but in relationship to our families, our cultures, our countries, and our ecological environments. Connectivity, relationship, and community are part and parcel of the human experience. We are beings in relationship with other beings!

In addition to interconnectedness, initiation is also an ever-present facet of the human experience. We did not choose to be born, at least not in any conventional sense. Our parents and God made that choice for us. We did not teach ourselves how to be human. Rather, we were initiated into the human family by our parents and their ethnic, religious, class, and cultural roots. Who we are in every way is a reflection of these relationships and influences. Ultimately, the quality of our lives is determined by the quality of what is exchanged, given, and received from our parents, our societies, and our many relationships.

Into the Stream of Grace

The dynamics of interconnectedness and initiation are not only true on human physical and psychological levels, but also in the spiritual realm. Just as we do not make the decision to be born or initiated into a particular family or culture, likewise we do not initiate ourselves into the consciousness of divine life of our own volition. We are brought into the stream of grace in and through others, most especially through the blessing of the guru. The role of a guru can be a blow to our modern sensibilities, our exaggerated sense of independence, and our misguided notions of equality. We are all equal in human dignity and equally deserving of human rights, but we are not equal in our abilities and certainly not in terms of spiritual evolution! Though we all have the capacity to experience absolute union with God, not many of us have reached the fullness of God-realization. We are all in a state of fallen consciousness, and we all need a helping hand. Saint Bonaventure explores this truth as he writes, "And just as, when one has fallen, he must lie where he is unless someone join him and lend a hand to raise him up, so our soul could not be perfectly lifted up and out of these things of sense to see itself and the eternal Truth in itself had not Truth, taking on human form in Christ, become a ladder restoring the first ladder that had been broken in Adam."[53]

An authentic teacher never represents him or herself, but rather a lineage of God-realized masters and their inspired teachings. When a devotee embraces Kriya Yoga, he or she stands on the shoulders of our Gurus, guided by their wisdom and protected by their grace. We never travel to God alone. In truth, we are surrounded by a cloud of loving witnesses! In the following paragraphs, let us pause to look with respect and love at the gurus of the Kriya Yoga lineage.

Jesus Christ

Yogananda taught, "Jesus Christ is very much alive and active today... With his all-embracing love he is not content to merely enjoy his blissful consciousness in heaven. He is very much concerned about mankind and wishes to give his followers the means to attain divine freedom of entry into God's infinite kingdom."[54] Jesus belongs not only to Christians, but to the entire world. His love extends to all people, regardless of cast or creed. Yogananda very much believed that his mission to the West was blessed by Jesus. He described his mission in this way: "To reestablish God in the temples of souls through revival of

---

54. St. Bonaventure, *The Journey of the Mind to God*, 23.
54. Paramahansa Yogananda, *The Second Coming*, xxvii

the original teachings of God-communion as propounded by Christ and Krishna is why I was sent to the West." Yogananda also stated, "Babaji is ever in communion with Christ; together they send out vibrations of redemption and have planned the spiritual technique of salvation for this age."[55]

Mahavatar Babaji

Nothing is known about the birth and life of Mahavatar Babaji, who reveals himself to very few. The deathless avatar resides in remote regions of the Himalayan Mountains in India. When he revived the lost meditation technique known as Kriya Yoga through his beloved disciple Lahiri Mahasaya, he told him, "The cries of many bewildered worldly men and women have not fallen unheard on the ears of the Great Ones. You have been chosen to bring spiritual solace through Kriya Yoga to numerous earnest seekers. The millions who are encumbered by family ties and heavy worldly duties will take new heart from you, a householder like themselves. You should guide them to understand that the highest yogic attainments are not barred to the family man. Even in the world, the yogi who faithfully discharges his responsibilities, without personal motive or attachment, treads the sure path of enlightenment."[56] Just before Yogananda came to America in 1920, Mahavatar Babaji appeared to him, saying, "Follow the behest of your guru and go to America. Fear not; you shall be

---

55. Ibid., xxviii
56. Paramahansa Yogananda, *Autobiography*, 275.

protected. You are the one I have chosen to spread the message of Kriya Yoga in the West."[57] Ultimately, Babaji guides the spiritual evolution of all devotees of Kriya Yoga. When we reverently mention his name, we receive an immediate blessing.

Lahiri Mahasaya

Lahiri Mahasaya was born on September 30, 1828, in the village of Ghurni in Bengal, India. Lahiri's guru Mahavatar Babaji appeared to him while he was hiking in the Himalayan foothills near Ranikhet. In fact, their meeting was a wonderfully blissful reunion in that they had been together in many lifetimes. Immediately, Mahavatar Babaji initiated Lahiri in the ancient path of Kriya Yoga and gave him the task of bestowing the sacred technique on all sincere seekers. From his simple home in Banaras, Lahiri Mahasaya initiated many devotees into the practices of Kriya Yoga. He was the first to teach the lost science of Kriya Yoga in modern times. Truly a groundbreaking figure in the renewal of Yoga within India, his influence spans the globe. Yogananda says, "As the fragrance of flowers cannot be suppressed, so Lahiri Mahasaya, quietly living as an ideal householder, could not hide his innate glory. Devotee-bees from every part of India began to seek the divine nectar of the liberated master....The harmoniously balanced life of the great householder-guru became the inspiration of thousands of men and women."[58] Yogananda's par-

---

57. Ibid., 303.
58. Ibid., 283.

ents were devout disciples of Lahiri Mahasaya, and when Yogananda was born they brought him to the great guru for a blessing. At that moment, Lahiri predicted, "Thy son will be a yogi. As a spiritual engine, he will carry many souls to God's kingdom."[59] Clearly, his prediction came to pass. Lahiri Mahasaya left his body on September 26, 1895, but sincere practitioners of Kriya Yoga can experience his bliss-filled consciousness. The gurus remain available to devotees even after they have left the body. *Autobiography of a Yogi* includes a fascinating and inspiring account of Lahiri Mahasaya's life.

Swami Sri Yukteswar

Swami Sri Yukteswar, Yogananda's guru, was born on May 10, 1855, at Serampore in Bengal, India. He was a direct disciple of Lahiri Mahasaya and is considered to have attained the spiritual stature of an incarnation of wisdom. Very interested in the synthesis of the Eastern and Western traditions, Sri Yukteswar believed that such a synthesis could alleviate much suffering in the world. When he had a life-changing encounter with Mahavatar Babaji in 1894, Babaji asked, "At my request, will you not write a short book on the underlying harmony between Christian and Hindu scriptures? Their basic unity is now obscured by men's sectarian differences. Show by parallel references that the inspired sons of God have spoken the same truths."[60] A short time later, Sri Yukteswar

---

59. Ibid., 16.
60. Ibid., 294.

wrote the *The Holy Science*, showing that the teachings of Jesus are totally aligned with the truths proclaimed in the Vedas. Babaji also told Sri Yukteswar, "You, Swamiji, have a part to play in the coming harmonious exchange between Orient and Occident. Some years hence I shall send you a disciple whom you can train for yoga dissemination in the West. The vibrations of many spiritually seeking souls come floodlike to me. I perceive potential saints in America and Europe, waiting to be awakened."[61] Paramahansa Yogananda was that disciple to whom Babaji referred. At their first meeting, Sri Yukteswar told Yogananda, "My son, you are the disciple that, years ago, Babaji promised to send me."[62] Swami Sri Yukteswar perfectly prepared Yogananda for his mission to the West. He left his body on March 9, 1936 while Yogananda was visiting in India.

Paramahansa Yogananda

From Babaji and Jesus, to Lahiri Mahasaya and then to Swami Sri Yukteswar, Paramahansa Yogananda was given the tremendous task of disseminating Kriya Yoga to the West, indeed to the whole world. Though he left his body in 1952, he continues to lead countless souls into ever deepening levels of God-communion. Yogananda is very present to all sincere devotes. From personal experience, I can attest to the power of his grace-filled presence. He is and will forever be the Sat-Guru of The Assisi Institute. Yoga-

---

61. Ibid.
62. Ibid.

nanda's blessing inspires us in every way, and his teachings are a perfect guide for modern men and women who desire to know God intimately. It should be noted that shortly before he left his body, Yogananda stated that he was the last guru in the Kriya lineage. There are and will be inspired teachers to represent our lineage, but no more gurus.

We, Too, Are Interconnected and Initiated

My first teacher of Kriya Yoga was Roy Eugene Davis. Born in 1931, Roy became a direct disciple of Yogananda at the young age of 18; his teaching years began upon his ordination in 1951 and continue to this day. A prolific author, his books are published in many languages, and he counts lovers of God from all over the world among his students. Roy is a man of impeccable character, deep realization, and sincere humility. When I attended one of his week-long retreats in 2002, he surprised me when he gave me permission to teach Kriya Yoga and to represent the Kriya lineage. A number of years later he formally ordained me and gave me his permission to integrate the Kriya tradition with mystical Christianity in my own teaching, thus blessing the mission of The Assisi Insititute. Roy, who is the last of Yogananda's disciples who still teaches publically, offers blessings to devotees by his very presence.

When Roy initiated me into Kriya Yoga, I became keenly aware of Yogananda's presence and blessing, and at that moment I felt the intuition that I was being initiated into something very sacred and much larger than myself. Since that time, my awareness of the gurus' presence in my life has only deepened. Three years later when Roy ordained me, my experience of the guru lineage deepened. I knew that my ministry was not to be about me, but to represent the lineage of our tradition. It was and continues to be both awe-inspiring and very humbling. When I have the privilege of initiating others into the path of Kriya Yoga, I have the awareness of acting as an empty channel for the flow of the gurus' grace. As blissfully profound as the initiation experience is, I have the realization that it really has nothing to do with me.

When people are initiated into Kriya Yoga at The Assisi Institute, they may feel drawn to one of the gurus in our lineage other than Yogananda. For example, certain individuals from a strongly Christian background will know that Jesus is their primary guru, which is perfectly acceptable in the spirit of what Yogananda taught. Some initiates are devoted to the Blessed Mother or Anandamayi Ma. This is acceptable as long as they are also committed to living the Kriya lifestyle and integrating the teachings of Yogananda into their understanding of God and the spiritual life. Among true gurus of the highest order, there is no competition! They all desire to bring their devotees home to the one God. A story about Lahiri Mahasaya from Yogananda's *Autobiography* perfectly illustrates the inclusive nature of Kriya Yoga: "The master encouraged his various disciples to adhere to the good traditional discipline of their own faiths. Stressing the all-inclusive nature of Kriya Yoga as a practical technique of liberation, Lahiri Mahasaya then gave his chelas liberty to express their lives in conformance with environment and upbringing. 'A Moslem should perform his namaz worship five times daily...several times daily a Hindu should sit in meditation... A Christian should go down on his knees several times daily, praying to God and then reading the Bible."[63]

Yogananda's Desire Mirrors Our Desire

In *Autobiography of a Yogi*, Paramahansa Yogananda describes in vivid detail his need and desire for a God-realized guru: "Torn by spiritual anguish, I entered the attic one dawn, resolved to pray until an answer was vouchsafed. 'Merciful Mother of the Universe, teach me Thyself through visions, or through a Guru sent by Thee!' The passing hours found my sobbing pleas without response. Suddenly I felt lifted as though bodily to a sphere uncircumscribed. 'Thy Master cometh today!' A divine womanly voice came from everywhere and nowhere."[64] What is curious about Yogananda's prayer was that he was already a spiritually developed person, steeped in moral living, prayer, and meditation. Yet he was humble enough to realize that without a God-realized guru he could not reach his full spiritual potential. May we be just as humble!

---

63. Ibid., 284.
64. Paramahansa Yogananda, *Autobiography*, 78.

Who is a God-Realized Guru?

So we may ask, who is a God-realized guru? Yogananda gives us the answer in clear and simple terms: "Unlike the false teacher who feeds his ego with the purloined adoration of his followers, the true spiritual shepherd – a God-knowing master, or guru – is a clear, pure channel, unobstructed by ego, relating to God all of the devotion of his disciples. To the true guru-shepherd, the Heavenly Porter opens the door to all divine secrecies, through which the guru leads his obedient, truth-seeking, meek, lamb-like followers... The guru bestows spiritual baptism on the devotee, by which God unlocks the entryway of the spiritual eye through which the devotee follows the 'voice' of the shepherd of Christ Consciousness to the Cosmic Consciousness of God. Only a true guru is empowered by God to establish with disciples a divine relationship by which he leads those in his care out of the common sheepfold of delusion to freedom in the Elysian pastures of God-consciousness."[65]

A bit of my own story may help to explain the need for the blessing of the guru. I was raised Catholic, and at the age of 16 I had a profound encounter with Christ. Yet as a young adult, I struggled to consistently stabilize my spiritual realizations. I prayed for guidance and for God to send me a spiritual mentor. Serendipitously, a colleague gave me the book *Autobiography of a Yogi* and suggested that I read it. Since my very first reading, Yogananda has been a spiritual father to me – a guru. Through his writings, spiritual presence, and intuitive guidance, I have become a bet-

---

65. Paramahansa Yogananda, *The Second Coming*, 1014 – 1015.

ter Christian. The sense of Christ's presence is more alive within me now than ever!

How is it possible that a Hindu monk from India brought me closer to Christ? The Christ Consciousness that permeated every thought, word, and action of Jesus was thoroughly at work within the life and mission of Paramahansa Yogananda. God has no step-children! The divine intelligence, the Logos, that Jesus perfectly embodied can work in and through any purified instrument. At the end of his life, Yogananda wrote of a vision he had of Jesus: "His eyes were the most beautiful, the most loving eyes I have ever seen. The whole universe I saw glistening in those eyes. They were infinitely changing, and with each transition of expression I intuitively understood the wisdom conveyed. In his glorious eyes I felt the power that upholds and commands the myriad worlds. As he gazed down at me, a Holy Grail appeared at his mouth. It descended to my lips and touched them; then went up again to Jesus. After a few moments of rapt silent communion, he said to me: 'Thou dost drink of the same cup of which I drink.'"[66]

A Relationship of Love

Our relationship with the guru begins with gratitude and grows to include the mutual exchange of deep love. Yogananda's own guru Sri Yukteswar writes, "Regard the guru with deep love. To keep company with the guru is not only to be in his physical pres-

---

66. Ibid., *Second Coming*, xxxii.

ence as this is sometimes impossible, but mainly to keep him in our hearts and to be one with him in principle and to attune our hearts with him."[67]

In other words, we must love the spiritual father or mother God has sent us! Love is a unifying force, bringing lover and beloved into communion and eventually into union. When the resurrected Jesus appeared to Peter, he did not ask Peter why he denied him three times. Rather, three times he asked Peter, "Do you love me?"[68] Peter's shame and guilt over his denial of Jesus kept him from experiencing his master's grace and mercy. Only love could reunite Peter's heart to Jesus' heart. Sri Yukteswar teaches us, "The heart's natural love is the principal requisite to attain a holy life."[69]

Our task is to hold the guru in our hearts with love, gratitude, reverence, and a desire to conform. Such love and desire create an energetic resonance between the guru and us. We are literally pulled into the gravitational field of their consciousness! We actually begin to think with them, to will with them, to imagine with them, and to discern with them. Their love becomes our love; their strength, our strength; and their wisdom, our wisdom. In due time, their presence becomes a palpably conscious force in our lives. When we call on them with humility and a desire to do the will of God, they respond. This is what Jesus meant when he said, "I am the vine; you are the branches. If you remain in me and I in you, you will bear much

67. Sri Yukteswar, *The Holy Science*, 8ᵗʰ ed. (Los Angeles, CA: Self-Realization Fellowship, 1990), 60.
68. John 21:15–17.
69. Sri Yukteswar, *The Holy Science*, 56.

fruit; apart from me you can do nothing."[70]

Keeper of the Soul

The purpose of the guru's presence in the life of a disciple runs deeper still. To begin with, the guru guards the memory of our identity in God and the ultimate purpose of all of our successive lifetimes. He or she acts as "a perpetual memento ...with regard to the eternal mission assigned to the soul in the cosmic symphony, and with regard to the special room for the soul 'in my Father's house, where there are many rooms' (John 14:2). If it is necessary (the guru) awakens recollections of the soul's previous earthly lives, in order to establish continuity of endeavor – of the quest and aspiration of the soul from life to life - so that particular lives are not merely isolated episodes but constitute the stages of a single path towards one sole end."[71]

Perhaps a personal experience would be helpful here. The first time I visited Assisi, Italy, I was particularly moved by the spiritual energy in the chapel of San Damiano, the place where Francis heard Jesus speak to him from the cross. While meditating there, I had a profound sense of having lived in Assisi in a previous life. The very soil of Assisi felt like home! I sensed that my mother in this life was my mother in that previous life. Interestingly, I did not even believe in reincarnation at that time! The knowledge came

---

70. John 15:5.
71. Valentin Tomberg, *Meditations on the Tarot* (New York: Penguin Group, 1985), 376.

over me like a profound intuition, shattering my limited perceptions. More importantly, this experience was the beginning of my attempt to marry Franciscan spirituality with Kriya Yoga. Not coincidentally, Yogananda once referred to Saint Francis as his patron saint. On that day in Assisi, God and guru resurrected a past-life memory so that I could integrate it with my present life's mission.

The Guru Supports Us

In addition to guarding our soul's purpose, the guru cherishes our sincere longing for God. He or she knows that the disciple will experience times of weakness wherein the spirit is willing but the flesh is weak. In those moments, the guru is with us, praying for us, inspiring us. "This means to say that he fills in the breaks in the psychic functional organism...and makes up for the soul's failings – given the soul's good will towards it."[72] We see the guru's loving support beautifully played out in the relationship between Jesus and Peter, who was also called Simon. Once again we return to Peter's denial of Jesus. Though Peter had the best of intentions, he was about to deny Jesus, his guru, three times – and Jesus knew it. Jesus said to him, "Simon, behold, Satan has demanded permission to sift you like wheat; but I have prayed for you, Simon, that your faith may not fail. And when you have turned back, strengthen your brothers."[73]

---

72. Ibid.
73. Luke 22:31–32.

When needed, the guru makes his or her presence known in a way that is both clear and practical, to warn, inform, and give assurance. Many years ago when I was experiencing steep opposition to my work, I prayed for help. While sleeping one night, I woke to the sound of Yogananda's voice. Three times I heard him call my name. In the morning, my wife told me of a lucid dream she had. She told me that Yogananda instructed her to say, "Tell Craig not to worry. I am taking care of everything."

The Guru Defends Us

Perhaps most importantly, the guru defends us against karma! Karma is the law of cause and effect; it is the energetic trajectory upon which our lives unfold. In Catholic circles karma is the equivalent of divine justice. As well, karma is a biblical concept. Saint Paul tells us, "Be not deceived. God is not mocked: whatever you sow, you shall reap."[74] In the Kriya tradition, it is taught that when people are initiated into Kriya Yoga, fifty percent of their karma is removed. Yogananda's teaching is not superstitious magic, but scientific magic.

Even on a purely human level, we know that if we take people who are psychologically dysfunctional and place them within a truly healthy and supportive community, their functioning begins to improve even without any formal therapy. Why? Because they are absorbed into the habits and the loving energy of that

---

74. Galatians 6:7.

system. Their consciousness is, so to speak, metabolized into the gravitational consciousness of the healthy community. Mental health is not only taught, but caught!

What is true below is true above. Initiation into Kriya Yoga includes a beautiful laying on of hands ceremony which is far more than a pleasant ritual. The laying on of hands transmits an attunement to the lineage of the Kriya gurus. This attunement aligns us to their elevated energy and God-Consciousness. If received with sincerity, Kriya initiation baptizes us into a higher and more subtle vibration which alters our life's trajectory and transforms our karmic thumbprint. God's grace trumps karma – if we avail ourselves of it!

Perhaps it is helpful to think of the guru as a mother defending her child against the vicissitudes of karma. What did Jesus say as he was suffering in agony on the cross? "Father, forgive them, for they know not what they do."[75] So protective are the gurus of us that they even choose to absorb into themselves our negative energy, metabolizing it into their own consciousness and turning the water of our afflictions into the wine of the Spirit. We see this protectiveness in the Jewish scriptures where Moses said to the Lord after the children of Israel worshipped a god made of gold instead of the living God, "But now, if you will forgive their sin – and if not, blot me, I pray to Thee, out of the book of life which Thou has written."[76]

---

75. Luke 23:34.
76. Exodus 32:32.

We must remember that in order for the grace of the gurus to be an actual force in our lives, we must cooperate with it, using our free will and our capacity to love in order to avail ourselves of the treasures they offer. We must attune ourselves to their ever-present presence! The night before he died, Jesus gave his disciples this sage advice: "Remain in me, as I also remain in you. No branch can bear fruit by itself; it must remain in the vine. Neither can you bear fruit unless you remain in me."[77]

Open to the Guru's Grace

Many years ago, a Catholic priest gave me some simple but profound advice. He told me: "When you wake up in the morning, get on your knees and thank God for one more day, and ask Jesus to guide you through the day, to give you the wisdom and strength you need to live well." Over the years, I have modified his advice a bit. The first thing I do every morning is meditate. But before I begin my meditation practice, I ask Jesus and Yogananda to guide my meditation and my day and to help me to live in the flow of God's will. Through this simple practice, I nurture my conscious contact with the gurus. If I get lost in my day-to-day responsibilities, I breathe and come back to this simple invocation. It works!

Some question whether or not a deceased saint or spiritual master is still present to his or her disciples. My personal experience tells me that they are present

---

77. John 15:4.

to the degree that we are aware of their presence. As an ultimate source of authority, I turn to both Jesus and Yogananda. Jesus said, "Behold, I am with you, even to the end of the world."[78] Yogananda taught, "It is an erroneous assumption of limited minds that great ones such as Jesus, Krishna, and other divine incarnations are gone from the earth when they are no longer visible to human sight. This is not so. When a liberated master has dissolved his body in Spirit and yet manifests in form to receptive devotees, as Jesus has appeared throughout the centuries since his passing, such as to St. Francis, Saint Teresa, and many others of East and West, it means he has an ongoing role to play in the destiny of the world. Even when Masters have completed their specific role for which they took on a physical incarnation, it is the divinely ordained task of some to look after the welfare of humanity and assist in guiding its progress."[79]

In addition to prayerful devotion, there are other ways to nurture our conscious contact with the guru. Kriya Yoga teaches us another essential practice: the contemplation of the words of Jesus and Yogananda. The concept of *contemplation* holds great importance in many spiritual traditions. The yogic concept of meditation is parallel to the Christian understanding of contemplative prayer. So what do we mean by contemplation? The term comes from the Latin "comtemplari," which means "to observe," or "to gaze on" – but contemplation is much deeper than mere observation or a casual glance. Contemplation means that we gaze upon something with naked or pure intention,

---

78. Matthew 28:20.
79. Paramahansa Yogananda, *The Second Coming*, xxvii.

allowing it to reveal itself to us. Eventually, we become one with – or are absorbed into – the object of
our contemplation. For now, let us begin with using
contemplation as a means of contact with the guru.

When we contemplate the words of the guru in holy
scripture, we are not analyzing their meaning in some
philosophical or theological way. Rather, we are con-
necting with the God-inspired consciousness that
gave birth to everything they said. When we approach
contemplation in this simple and prayerful way, we
are availing ourselves of the gurus' energetic force
field, which will elevate our consciousness.

Contemplating the gurus' divinely inspired words is a
simple practice. We take a phrase or two and prayerfully repeat it a number of times, allowing our awareness to be metabolized into its truth. The prayerful
contemplation of a great truth, which acts upon us as
a healing balm, has the power to purify both our
minds and our emotions. For this reason Jesus said,
"You shall know the truth and the truth will set you
free."[80] Truth liberates! One of my favorite passages to
contemplate is this truth from Jesus: "Do not let your
hearts be troubled. You believe in God; believe also in
me."[81]

We can easily take contemplation into our daily activities. Imagine how different our psychological,
emotional, and day-to-day lives would be if periodically we came back to a quote from Jesus, Yogananda,
or another great saint! Though it takes effort to inte-

80. John 8:32.
81. John 14:1.

grate contemplation into our lives, the elevation of our consciousness into the consciousness of the guru is a pearl of infinite worth.

Another simple practice that effectively attunes our minds and hearts to the gurus' consciousness is the repetition of their names. When done with love and sincerity, the repetition of a holy name becomes a very powerful practice. Thomas of Celano, a follower and biographer of Francis of Assisi, tells us, "Francis was intimately united with Jesus – Jesus always in his heart, Jesus on his lips, Jesus in his ears, Jesus in his eyes, Jesus in his hands, Jesus in all the other members of his body. How many times he would be eating dinner and would hear mention of or think about Jesus and forget to eat... Often when he was on a journey, meditating or singing about Jesus, he would leave the road and start inviting all creatures to praise Jesus."[82] Likewise, Yogananda gives us a beautiful and effective mantra to practice during day-to-day activities, one that is very much in the spirit of Saint Francis' practice: "In waking, eating, working, dreaming, sleeping, serving, meditating, chanting, divinely loving, my soul constantly hums, unheard by any: God! Christ! Guru!"[83]

Finally, attunement to the guru also involves a willingness to incorporate the guru's principles into our lives and to contribute to the carrying out of his or her mission. Jesus never said "Worship me," but he

---

82. *365 St. Francis of Assisi*, 205.
83. Paramahansa Yogananda, *Man's Eternal Quest* (Los Angeles, CA: Self-Realization Fellowship, 2002), 463. Yogananda prayed two versions of this prayer. One is as above; the other repeats, "God! God! God! In *The Second Coming*, he explains that this prayer was inspired by a vision of St. Francis of Assisi.

did say, "Follow me."[84] We follow Jesus and Yogananda in the way of virtue and service. Quite literally, we become their voices in the world, their hands in the world, and their love in the world. A challenging calling? Yes! But this calling elevates us, ennobles us, and gives us a life worth living.

Ultimately, we become what we focus on, what we pay attention to, and what we love. To the extent that we truly love the guru, the guru's God-consciousness marries our consciousness, and our lives take on the fragrance of the guru's life. St. Francis of Assisi shows us what such a holy union of souls can be. Francis was so focused on Jesus and so wanted to imitate him that a few years before he died he became the world's first stigmatist, receiving the wounds of Jesus in his feet, hands, and side. In a manner of speaking, Francis became another Jesus.

An Eternal Relationship

Our relationship with the guru spans eternity. In life, in death, in the afterlife, and in subsequent lives, the guru remains at our side like a mother watching over her child. The guru is always with us! Yes, there are inspired teachers through whom God works and through whom God blesses. But only a guru of the highest order, a Sat-Guru, can take on our karma and commit to us in such a complete and total way. In life, no relationship is more important than the guru-disciple bond. A quote from Yogananda's *Autobiogra-*

---

84. Matthew 4:19.

phy perfectly captures the guru-disciple relationship. It is the meeting between Lahiri Mayasaya and his guru, the immortal Babaji. Babaji said to Lahiri, "For more than three decades I have waited for you to return to me... you slipped away and disappeared into the tumultuous waves of the life beyond death. The magic wand of your karma touched you, and you were gone! Though you lost sight of me, never did I lose sight of you. I pursued you over the luminescent astral sea where the glorious angels sail. Through gloom, storm, upheaval, and light I followed you, like a mother bird guarding her young. As you lived out your human term of womb life, and emerged a babe, my eye was ever on you. When you covered your tiny form in the lotus posture under the Ghurni sands in childhood, I was invisibly present. Patiently, month after month, year after year, I have watched over you, waiting for this perfect day. Now you are with me! Here is your cave, loved of yore; I have kept it ever clean and ready for you. Here is your hallowed asana blanket, where daily you sought to fill your expanding heart with God. Here is your bowl, from which you often drank the nectar prepared by me. See how I have kept the brass cup brightly polished, that someday you might drink again from it? My own, do you now understand?"

Lahiri replied, "My Guru, what can I say? Where has one ever heard of such depthless love?"[85]

At The Assisi Institute, we often contemplate the seven "I am" statements of Jesus from John's Gospel. Each of these underscores the role of the guru in the

---

85. Paramahansa Yogananda, *Autobiography*, 271.

life of a disciple, and because each is calibrated to one of the seven chakras, we also bring our attention to each successive chakra as we "breathe in" its energy and meaning. This is a form of Christian Kriya!

First Chakra: "I am the true vine." (John 15:1)

Second Chakra: "I am the way, the truth, and the life." (John 14:6)

Third Chakra: "I am the gate." (John 10:9)

Fourth Chakra: "I am the bread of life." (John 6:35)

Fifth Chakra: "I am the good shepherd." (John 10:11)

Sixth Chakra: "I am the light of the world." (John 8:12)

Seventh Chakra: "I am the resurrection and the life." (John 11:25)

Every great teacher or guru leaves behind a practice or a pathway for his or her disciples to evolve spiritually. Yogananda was no exception. He bequeathed to his future followers a system of spiritual practice, or asanas, that prepare the body, mind, and soul to absorb more and more divine energy. In the following chapter, I will share an overview of Kriya Yoga meditation as taught by Yogananda.

5 KRIYA YOGA MEDITATION

To be born a human being is indeed a great gift because God has fashioned us into the divine image. We are not meant to walk the earth as rational animals but as gods, arm in arm with the living God. According to Saint Bonaventure, we have been created "to see what is most beautiful, to hear what is most harmonious, to smell what is most fragrant, to taste what is most sweet, and to embrace what is most delightful."[86] Yes, we have a noble calling!

But clearly something has gone wrong. We are not living fully from our divine inheritance, from our actual identity in God, and instead we live our lives from a place of mistaken identity – from the egoic personality and all of its impulses. In this state of forgetfulness, we will necessarily create suffering for our-

---

86. St. Bonaventure, *The Journey of the Mind to God*, 24.

selves and others. Perhaps a personal story will help to bring home this truth. In my early thirties, I was involved in a twelve-step support group for children of alcoholics. My meditation teacher advised me, "I am glad you are attending these meetings and learning how your father's alcoholism impacted you, but don't define yourself as a child of an alcoholic." When I asked him why, he answered, "Because at your deepest level you are God's image. Don't limit yourself by identifying yourself with anything that is beneath your God-given dignity. Acknowledge your personality's wounds and compulsions, but never forget that you are not your personality."

When our attention is completely absorbed in the personality, the five senses, or the external play of creation, we cannot enter our own souls. We are estranged, practically speaking, from ourselves and God. Yogananda tells us, "Identifying himself with a shallow ego, man takes for granted that it is he who thinks, wills, feels, digests meals, and keeps himself alive, never admitting that in his ordinary life he is a puppet of past actions (karma) and of Nature or environment. Lofty above such influences, however, is his regal soul."[87] Kriya Yoga is a liberating path because it frees us from what Yogananda refers to as our "ego-prison"[88] by teaching us how to withdraw our attention and life-force from identification with the personality and its many desires, and by grounding our awareness in the soul, in God.

---

87. Paramahansa Yogananda, *Autobiography*, 214.
88. Ibid., 213.

Without a consistent meditation practice it is virtually impossible to wake up to our identity in God or to stabilize our spiritual realizations. Meditation, practiced with devotion, allows our interior consciousness to rise up and become a stream flowing into the spiritual world which elevates us above instinct, habit, and karma. Sri Yukteswar is quite clear about the fruit of proper meditation: "Man becomes again baptized or absorbed in the stream of Spiritual Light, and rising above the creation of darkness, enters into the spiritual world and becomes unified with the Son of God, as was the case with Lord Jesus of Nazareth."[89]

Mediation and our Humanity

We go to God not as angels or as disembodied souls, but as human beings with a body and a marvelously complex nervous system. Spiritual realization is a dynamic process that involves the subtle interaction between body and mind, spirit and soul. Let me share with you another story from that dark time in my life thirty years ago. One night in particular I was experiencing a deep level of despair. Not knowing what to do, I remembered a form of the Jesus Prayer that a friend taught me. I sat up straight with my head and neck gently aligned and my feet touching the floor. I steadied my breath to a calm and consistent pace. While focusing on my heart center, I mentally said the name of Jesus on my in-breath. Then I paused for a second, and on my out-breath I mentally prayed, "Have mercy on me." After about 45 minutes, my de-

---

89. Sri Yukteswar, *The Holy Science*, 42.

spair lifted and I rested in a state of deep peace. I had meditated before, but never with such a level of focus. This experience made me realize that there is a necessary discipline to meditation. How and why did my meditation in that dark moment bring me to peace? I believe there are several levels to the answer. To begin with, physical posture can impact our mood. Sitting in a dignified way helped me to be more alert and to feel stronger and more grounded. Secondly, the steadying of my breath helped to increase the flow of oxygen into my body, which reduced my physical tension and lowered the level of adrenaline pumping into my nervous system. A steady breath necessarily steadies the mind! Thirdly, placing my attention on my heart center had a double effect: it quieted my noisy mind by moving my attention into my body, and it opened my heart, which increased the flow of endorphins into my nervous system. Fourthly, by focusing my mind on the Jesus Prayer, my rumination ceased and I was eventually brought back to that present moment. Lastly and perhaps most importantly, I invoked the sacred name of Jesus. Saying his name with attention, love, and devotion opened me up to his energy and vibration – which created a positive shift in my own consciousness. In these next few pages I will take you through the meditation process as taught at The Assisi Institute. I invite you to join me!

Posture and Breath

Science has shown that there is a clear relationship between the mind and the body. Yes, the mind surely impacts the body, but the body also impacts the mind. A sleepy posture induces sleepiness, and a straight and strong posture produces concentration and alertness. It is that simple! In that spirit, we avoid passive sitting in the Kriya Yoga tradition. We sit comfortably poised and upright, with our head, neck, and spine gently aligned. Not only does this posture help with concentration, but it also helps to facilitate the flow of divine energy up and down the spiritual spine.

Once we are comfortably sitting in a meditative posture, we turn our attention to the breath. Breath and consciousness are intimately linked! For example, when we are anxious, angry, or frustrated, our breathing is typically quick, uneven, and jagged. Of course, this kind of breathing only makes our emotional state worse, because it increases the flow of adrenaline into our system and reduces the amount of oxygen in the body, thus creating even more anxiety, anger, and frustration. By contrast, when we are peaceful and focused, our breathing is naturally steadier and slower. By learning to steady the breath, we steady the mind and all its emotions. In the beginning of creation, Adam and Eve and all of humanity consciously breathed from the depths of their souls. Our spiritual ancestors lived and breathed God! This living and breathing of God is the very source of our existence, our lives, and our aliveness. We have forgotten how to breathe in this spiritual way and lost much of our conscious contact with God. Valentin Tomberg explains, "Originally, breathing was different from what it has become now. In a certain sense, it was total. It was vertical, comprised of both prayer and meditation, and horizontal, that is, the breathing in and out of air containing the 'vitamins' of life-force or prana."[90] It is interesting to note that in the biblical language of Hebrew, the word for *breath* is also the same word for *spirit*. Therefore, to breathe with awareness is to pray! In John's account of Pentecost, we are told that "Jesus breathed on his disciples and said, 'Receive the Holy Spirit.'"[91]

Kriya Yoga teaches us how to reclaim this God-given gift of conscious, soulful breathing. Accordingly, meditation always begins with the steadying of the breath. Gently, we deepen and steady the breath, breathing more from the diaphragm. Then we pause a second or two between inhalation and exhalation. Finally, we exhale in the same slow and deep manner. This type of breathing brings more oxygen into the body and helps to release tension as it quiets the mind. Master the breath and we master the mind! And this form of yogic breathing can be done virtually any time or any place – whenever it is needed.

Breath and Prana

It is important to mention here the Sanskrit word *prana* and its relationship to breath. Although there is no exact translation of *prana* into English, its most accurate translation is *life-force*. Prana is the life-force that enlivens and energizes our bodies, our emotions, our desires, our minds, our wills, and our spirits.

---

90. Valentin Tomberg, *Lazarus,* 272.
91. John 20:22.

Prana is imprinted with memory and will move according to our karmic imprints. For example, if people tend to be innately anxious or angry, the prana will habitually feed and prolong these states of being. Conversely, if people tend to be calm and optimistic, the prana will stimulate the part of the limbic system that produces feel-good hormones.

Though breath and prana are not one and the same, they are intimately linked; therefore, steadying the breath also steadies the flow of prana. Steadying prana is the first step toward mastering prana and ultimately, all of the rest of our lives. For example, by steadying my breath and placing my attention on the third eye, I am redirecting my prana to my "higher brain" which calms my emotions and brings clarity and perspective to my thought process. In Kriya Yoga, mastery of prana or life-force is called *pranayama*. I will explain more about pranayama later in the chapter. For now, Yogananda tells us, "Control of the senses is vitally linked to control of the prana or life force energy in the body – an intelligent, electric-like medium whose instrumentality enlivens the whole human mechanism...Prana holds the key to the bodily dwelling and to its inner apartments of the brain and consciousness. It lets in or shuts out all welcome or unwelcome visitors of sensations and actions, according to the guidance it receives or the free reign it is allowed."[92]

---

92. Paramahansa Yogananda, *The Bhagavad Gita*, 301.

Breath, Third Eye Focus, and Mantra

After we have settled into our meditative body posture and yogic breathing, we proceed by placing our attention on a specific point within the body or spinal column. Typically, in Kriya meditation, attention is on the third eye, the point between the eyebrows. As the third eye opens, our concentration deepens and our awareness begins to transcend our typically myopic perceptions. As our consciousness expands, our vision for our lives becomes clearer. As our intuitive capacities grow, we begin to see reality as God sees reality. In truth, there is only one seeing, one perceiving, and one consciousness – not ours, but God's. When Jesus said, "Whatever you do to the least of my brothers and sisters you do unto me,"[93] he was not simply encouraging us to behave better! He was sharing his consciousness: his way and God's way of seeing and experiencing reality. Ultimately, Jesus was inviting us to open the spiritual eye of our consciousness so that we too could see as he sees and share in his divine life. And for the Kriya Yogi, this expansion of sight – of consciousness – begins with the humble practice of focusing on the third eye.

While focusing on the third eye, we introduce a sacred mantra, a word that carries a holy or elevating vibration. In the Book of Genesis, God's creative activity was mediated through sacred words. "God said, 'Let there be light,' and there was light."[94] All words and sounds are vibrations. Our bodies are constantly vibrating; in fact, our bodies are nothing other than

---

93. Matthew 25:40.
94. Genesis 1:3.

vibrations of energy. The vibrations of the words that we say or think, therefore, interact with our bodies, our emotions, and our very consciousness, impacting us in a positive or negative manner. On a certain level, we are what we choose to think and feel! The Book of Proverbs says, "As a man thinks in his heart, so he is."[95]

Thus, a sacred mantra is not merely a word that gathers our attention towards a singular focus. More importantly, a mantra is a transformative vibration or sound imbued with the energy of God's Spirit. A mantra spoken regularly and sincerely will imprint our prana, literally divinizing the life-force that sustains us. Therefore, mantras purify the mind and work to elevate us above ego-consciousness, propelling us toward God-Consciousness. Valentin Tomberg writes, "In this case the breath becomes an organ for harmonizing with or participation in the Divine breath – the breathing of the breath of life, which is the kernel of the human being, eternally coming into being from God. For, God is eternal Being. And the true human Self of man is eternally coming into being as the breath of life from eternal Being. The Self of the human being rests in the breath of the Godhead – the breath that bestows being. In spiritualizing and raising up breathing to the highest level, humans experience the true Self as a star in the heaven of God's eternal Being."[96]

Just a few nights before I wrote this chapter, Vicki and I experienced a torrential rainfall at our home at 2

---

95. Proverbs 23:7.
96. Tomberg, *Lazarus*, 275.

a.m. Water was pooling against the back wall of the house just in front of sliding glass doors, threatening to flood our finished basement. Vicki and I were frantically bailing water outside in the pouring rain. I could feel the prana feeding my tendency towards anger, and a part of me really wanted to scream in frustration. But even while I dragged garbage pails filled with water to our side yard, I instinctively steadied my breath and internally repeated the Lord's Prayer. Instead of being washed away in a tide of unproductive anger, my mood remained steady and I actually began to feel an interior calm. And I must admit that I had even more spiritual help. When the rain storm was at its peak, my 88-year-old father-in-law pulled out his old Catholic prayer book and began praying a traditional prayer "for use during times of duress." Within minutes, the rain stopped!

We teach three particularly effective mantras at The Assisi Institute. The first, from Yogananda's teaching, is *Hong Sau*, pronounced *Hong Saw*. Hong Sau meditation, simple and powerful, induces deep peace. While seated in a meditative posture and having calmed the mind through the steadying of breath, we mentally repeat *Hong* on inhalation, pause, and mentally repeat *Sau* on exhalation, all while keeping our attention on the third eye. Breathing should be steady but gentle. The Hong Sau mantra should be continued until there is a sense of peace or stillness. Then, let the mantra go while allowing yourself to be absorbed into the peace. You may be aware of some mental background noise or conversation. Just let it be, while simultaneously attending to God's peace. If the mind begins to wander too much, just come back to the breath and the mantra until you feel calm once again.

The second mantra that Yogananda taught is the *Om* (or *Aum*) technique. Interestingly, Yogananda associates the Om mantra with the presence of the Holy Spirit. He writes, "The vibratory force emanating from Spirit...is the Holy Ghost: Cosmic Vibration, the Word, *Aum* (Om), or Amen."[97] In other words, the mantra Om is a vibration arising from God's loving Spirit; it contains and expresses the creative and life-sustaining energy of God and serves as a portal to conscious contact with the Holy Spirit.

The Om technique is very simple: while sitting in the meditative posture and focusing on the third eye, inhale slowly; while pausing, mentally say *Om*, and then exhale. Continue to repeat this procedure. Some people speak of hearing subtle noise in the inner ear that sounds like different musical notes, quietly roaring thunder, or a buzzing beehive. If these sounds arise, just allow yourself to merge with them. But much more important than hearing any sounds is the process of being absorbed in That which gives birth to these sounds: the Divine Presence, experienced as enlivened Wholeness, as liberating Power, as the Comforter, as Love. Just before his death, Jesus spoke of the coming of the Comforter: "The Comforter, the Holy Spirit, whom the Father will send in my name, will teach you all things and will remind you of everything I have said to you. Peace I leave with you; my peace I give you. I do not give to you as the world gives. Do not let your hearts be troubled and do not

---

97. Paramahansa Yogananda, *The Second Coming*, 11.

be afraid."[98]

Yogananda tells us that by meditating on Om, we avail ourselves of the energy and fruits of the Spirit: "The uplifting vibrations of 'The Comforter' bring profound inner peace and joy. The Creative Vibration vitalizes the individual life force in the body, which conduces to health and well-being, and can be consciously directed as healing power to those in need of divine aid. Being the source of intelligent creativity, the *Aum* vibration inspires one's own initiative, ingenuity, and will."[99]

The last mantra that I want to discuss is the *Jesus Prayer*, which has its origins in the monasteries of sixth-century Sinai and Mount Athos, the spiritual capital of Orthodox Christianity in Greece. Before getting into the details of this mantra, I want to reflect on the importance of a *name* in Judeo-Christian thought. A name is more than a label that is given to someone. According to Jean-Yves, Leloup, "In Semitic thought a name designates in a general way the hidden nature of something, a sort of active presence. To know someone by name is to know his or her depths and to hold power over them. Hence, to know the name of God is to have power."[100] In other words, in a person's name we find his or her mission, energy, and consciousness. The Jesus Prayer, when done with sincerity and devotion, opens us to the very consciousness of Christ. The Jesus Prayer is this simple sentence: *Lord Jesus Christ, son of God, have mercy on*

98. John 14:27.
99. Paramahansa Yogananda, *Second Coming*, 124.
100. Jean-Yves Leloup, *Being Still: Reflections on an Ancient Mystical Tradition*, trans. M.S. Laird (New York/Mahwah, NJ: Paulist Press, 2003), 104.

me. When we say the Jesus Prayer, we focus not on the third eye, but the heart. With the inhaling breath, we mentally say, *Lord Jesus Christ, Son of God,* and then we pause for a second or two, and while exhaling say, *have mercy on me.* Asking Jesus for mercy is not an exercise in self-hatred or a form of self-pity, but something far greater. Leloup explains, *"Lord have mercy means You who are, send your Breath, your Spirit upon me and upon everyone, and we shall be renewed. Let your Compassion and Goodness be upon me and upon everyone. Do not consider my inability to love you or your world. Make my desire flourish. Turn my heart of stone into a heart of flesh."*[101] The Jesus Prayer avails us of all the love, grace, and wisdom that is in Christ. It is a font of unending goodness! When one's heart is opened and there is a sense of the Holy Spirit's presence, we can let go of both breath and mantra and just rest in the presence of Jesus. It is important to note that the Jesus Prayer can be practiced anytime, not just in meditation. Leloup quotes the anonymous author of *The Way of the Pilgrim,* who was a master of the Jesus Prayer: "Whenever someone insults me, I think of nothing but the gracious Jesus Prayer. Very soon the anger or pain subsides, and I forget all about it. I've become a bit odd: nothing really eats away at me; nothing worries me... By force of habit I have but one need: to recite unceasingly the Jesus Prayer and when I do it I am filled with peace."[102]

---

101. Ibid., 77.
102. Ibid., 82.

Kriya Pranyama

There is a powerful technique of meditation given during Kriya Initiation called *Kriya Pranyama* which brings us these blessings:

It helps to control and direct the flow of prana, life force, in a manageable, balanced way that maximizes physical, psychological, and spiritual health.

It directs the flow of prana through the seven chakras or spiritual centers, dissolving karmic patterns and cleansing the chakras.

It purifies the chakras in such a way that they become channels for divine energy and help to support our spiritual evolution.

It opens the higher chakras which enhance our spiritual perceptions.

It cauterizes habitual neural pathways in the brain, while simultaneously enhancing neural plasticity.

It effectively decreases beta waves in the brain, which are associated with anxiety, stress, and increased levels of adrenaline.

It increases alpha waves in the brain, which are associated with a sense of peace and relaxation. It also increases theta waves, which are related to a sense of creativity, emotional connectedness, intuition, and bliss.

Although the exact details of the Kriya technique can

only be given at the time of initiation, Yogananda gives us the following description: "The Kriya Yogi mentally directs his life energy to revolve, upward and downward, around the six spinal centers (chakras)... One-half minute of revolution of energy around the sensitive spinal cord of man effects subtle progress in his evolution."[103] Each upward breath or inhalation not only increases the level of prana moving up the spiritual spine, but also creates a form of a prayer wherein we offer all aspects of our humanity to God. Whatever is sincerely offered to God is lovingly received and blessed by God. And as we exhale, we draw down the Light of Christ, that pure luminous brilliance of the Spirit, through the crown chakra. As this Divine Energy moves through us, it helps to heal the nervous system and ultimately illumines and divinizes our consciousness. One of Yogananda's direct disciples, Norman Paulson, describes the effects of the Kriya Pranyama technique in this way: "As you turn the wheel of meditation, the Breath of Life begins to heal and dissolve thought-forms, your seeds of karma from this life and past lives. You begin to clean your temple out, opening up all of the inner-dimensional doors or gateways to the healing light of the Divine. . . As you meditate and draw nearer to God, all the seeds of your past actions and desires are transmuted, fulfilled or burned up and dissolved in the Breath of Life. The road to heaven indeed becomes a highway; your spiritual evolution is quickened. The transformation begins."[104] The Kriya Pranayama technique not only redistributes our prana in healthy and life-enhancing ways, but it also avails

---

103. Paramahansa Yogananda, *Autobiography*, 210.
104. Norman Paulson, *Sacred Science: Meditation, Transformation, Illumination* (Buellton, CA: The Solar Logos Foundation, 1998), 139.

us of God's presence in the form of what Orthodox Christians call *Uncreated Light*. Moses encountered this light in a burning bush; Jesus'disciples, on Mount Tabor at the Transfiguration. Though rare, it can be seen with the eye of the soul – the inner eye. But more important than actually seeing this light is the effect that it has on us: it purifies and illuminates our consciousness and gives us strength of will and right impulse. It divinizes our lives. The ultimate fruition of this light is perfectly expressed by Saint Isaac: "The spiritual person's heart is aflame with love for every creature, even for reptiles and demons."[105] Read the following words of Yogananda as he writes about Uncreated Light: "The body of the average man is like a fifty-watt lamp... Through gradual and regular increase of the simple and foolproof methods of Kriya, man's body becomes astrally transformed day by day, and is finally fitted to express those infinite potentials of cosmic energy that constitute the first materially active expression of Spirit."[106]

Perhaps a personal story will clarify the meaning and power of Uncreated Light. Recently I found myself in an agonizingly long line at the DMV due to my own procrastination. Through breathing and prayer, I managed to bring myself into a Buddhist-like state of detached calm, but the best was yet to come. When Vicki joined me on the bench and learned that we had a long wait ahead of us, she neither chastised me nor complained. With a joyful light radiating from her eyes, she simply said, "As long as we have to be here, why don't we just enjoy our time together?" At that

---

105. Leloup, *Being Still*, 66.
106. Paramahansa Yogananda, *Autobiography*, 211.

moment, joy washed over me. Together, we had a delightful time while we waited. Vicki's light, which has its origins in God, lifted my spirit. At the end of our wait, I told her that I would always remember this experience with her at the DMV. As a footnote to this story, the benches at the DMV are old church pews which came from SS. Peter and Paul Church, which was my boyhood church as well as the place where I served as pastoral administrator. The many memories embedded in those pews made my experience that day even more meaningful!

Devotion and Grace

Yogananda stated many times that the Kriya Yoga technique is only effective to the extent that it is energized with heartfelt devotion. Otherwise, it is just a mechanical technique and has no power to transform our lives. When the Kriya technique is yoked to our love for God, it is a very effective force in the process of our spiritual evolution. However, a technique, no matter how effective, is never an end in and of itself. By purifying our nervous systems and enlivening our spiritual perceptions, the Kriya technique brings us to the gate of the temple. But only grace can usher us into the temple, that is, into the experience of unadulterated union with God. Consider this parable: A spiritual master was walking along the beach one morning when he came across one of his students meditating. He asked, "Why are you meditating?"

The student replied, "To achieve God-realization, of course."

The master stated, "You can no more achieve God-realization than you can make the sun rise before it is ready to do so."

Irritated, the student asked, "Then why do you have me meditating every morning?"

The master said, "So that when the sun does rise you won't be asleep."

The best of techniques prepares us for the experience of meditation and should never be mistaken for the actual experience of God. Science tells us that nature abhors a vacuum, but God is most especially drawn to our emptiness, poverty, or deficiency. In fact, God's light is so bright that it initially blinds us, especially in relationship to our imagined enlightenment. Paradoxically, our darkness is the necessary preparation for the experience of God's light. God is never closer than when we are in darkness. The true mystic is the one who has learned to see in the dark!

Practical Considerations

Meditation at any time of the day is good, but it is best to meditate early in the morning, when the environment is quiet and settled.

Meditating at the same time of the day is recommended because the human psyche responds favorably to consistency.

A simple meditation routine can take as little as 20

minutes, especially in the beginning. It is recommended that at least one day a week, perhaps on a Sunday, one should meditate for a longer period of time so as to deepen the meditative experience. For those who have been initiated into Kriya Yoga, the recommendation is to meditate twice a day – in the morning and again in the evening before retiring.

Creating a space specifically designated for meditation is most helpful because space holds energy, especially sacred energy. And sacred energy supports us in our meditative efforts! Also, a space that is quiet and free from the interruptions of electronic devices is obviously conducive to meditation.

An altar with images of the gurus and favorite saints helps to create a spiritual environment and give us a supportive visual focus. Sacred images are literally windows into heavenly realms. There are times, for example, when I quietly gaze at an icon of Jesus or a photo of Yogananda, and this simple gazing becomes a form of meditation in itself as I am drawn into their consciousness.

The Meditation Process

Warmup: It helps to begin with some gentle breathing, perhaps some chanting or spiritual reading, and always with a prayer.

Preparatory technique: Though meditative techniques are never an end unto themselves, they prepare us to enter into the meditative experience. The preparatory technique sets the stage – it helps to calm the nervous system, focus our attention, and interiorize our awareness. When we have spent some time quieting ourselves with a technique, we are ready to enter into the meditation itself.

The meditation: Simply, meditation is a sense of loving communion with the Divine. Background thoughts can be present or not. Communion with the Divine is the simple experience of being absorbed in the sound or some other perception of Aum, light, joy, love, peace, or stillness. We must never think that we have exhausted the depth of God's presence. There is always a deeper realization! Yogananda writes, "Stillness is the altar of Spirit. There is no limit of the deepening of stillness. There is no limit of ever-new Joy. Never give mental boundaries to your perception of Joy...[There are] no depths to be reached; you must keep expanding in universal consciousness and keep deepening your apperception of ever-new, unending Bliss. He is the inexhaustible Bliss who will entertain us throughout eternity, without cessation."[107]

We must never underestimate the power of meditation to heal the mind and transform our consciousness! Meditation is literally a healing balm. I suggest you slowly read these words of the great medieval saint and mystic, Bernard of Clairvaux: "Meditation purifies the soul. Then it regulates the inclinations, directs activity, moderates excess, shapes morals, makes life honest and regulated, and mediates knowl-

---

107. *Rajarsi Janakananda: A Great Western Yogi* (Los Angeles, CA: Self-Realization Fellowship, 1994), 96.

edge of divine as well as human things. It is this which replaces confusion with order, checks the inclination to lose oneself in uncertainty, gathers together that which is disbursed, penetrates into that which is hidden, discovers that which is true and distinguishes it from that which merely appears as such, and brings to light fiction and lie. Further, it is meditation which determines beforehand what is to be done and which brings that which has been done to consciousness, so that nothing remains in the soul which is in need of clarification and correction. Likewise, it is meditation which enables misfortune to be foreseen even when happiness prevails and which, during misfortune, makes it possible to preserve an attitude of not being dejected. It is the source of courage on the one hand and of prudence on the other."[108]

Contemplation

At the end of a period of meditation, it is most beneficial to contemplate a sacred truth given to us by a great saint or spiritual master. Contemplation is not analysis, speculation, or mental consternation. Contemplation is opening our heart and mind to liberating truth. Just as meditation purifies the mind, contemplating truth purifies and settles the emotions. Truth creates an emotional life that is appropriately fluid, grace-filled, and rich in joy and gratitude. After resting in meditative silence for a period of time, simply repeat (most often internally) a sacred phrase three or four times. Then, take the contemplation

---

108. Bernard of Clairvaux, *De Consideratione* I,7.

with you into your day-to-day life. Two of my favorite contemplations from the Gospel of John are, "Do not let your hearts be troubled. You believe in God; believe also in me" (14:1), and, "Be of good cheer, I have overcome the world" (16:33).

Prayer

Yogananda often stated that the very best time to pray is at the end of meditation, when our awareness has been clarified and our prayers easily arise from the depths of our souls. At this time, our prayers are very powerful. Also, nothing strengthens the human will like prayer, because prayer is the lifting up of our minds and our hearts to God, uniting our prayerful wills to God's loving and all powerful will. In this moment, God literally wills with us, making our wills strong and indomitable! Of course, the most appropriate prayer is always one of gratitude.

A Way of Life

The ultimate goal of meditation is not more meditation, but union with God. Ultimately, meditation is not something we do, but a way of life, a way of perceiving, a way of relating, a way of experiencing, a way of loving God and others. For this reason Yogananda said again and again, "Read a little, meditate more, and think of God always."[109] At the deepest

---

109. Roy Davis, direct disciple of Yogananda, quoting the Master.

level, meditation is prayer, and prayer is meditation. And just as the spiritual life is not complete without meditation, neither is it complete without prayer. We will explore the meaning of prayer in the next chapter.

6 PRAYER

When I first began to practice Kriya Yoga, I found that meditation nurtured my spirit in profound ways. I was so taken with meditation that I virtually stopped praying altogether! But then I had a powerful dream while I was on a pilgrimage in Assisi, Italy. In my dream, an angelic figure asked me if I wanted to know how prayer worked. Of course I answered yes! He took me to a realm high above earth. Looking down, I could see columns of light rising up, and I also saw beams of light descending and merging with the ascending columns of light. The angelic figure asked me if I knew what was happening; I did not! Then he explained, "The ascending columns of light are people's sincere and heartfelt prayers rising toward heaven, and the descending beams of light are God's angels answering their prayers. This is how prayer works! I want you to tell others that their soulful prayers are heard and answered."

So our spiritual practices must include prayer! Before we explore prayer, though, it would be helpful for us to review what Yogananda taught about the difference between ego-consciousness and super-consciousness. The path of Kriya Yoga, as well as all the world's other mystical traditions, moves us in a very specific direction: from ego-consciousness to what Yogananda referred to as "super-consciousness." Under the sway of ego-consciousness we experience ourselves as being separate from God, isolated from the flow of heaven's generosity, and entirely on our own. Ego-consciousness is a recipe for a profound sense of inadequacy. We were never meant to live our lives separate from the immediate sense of God's loving support and provision!

By contrast, super-consciousness is not an otherworldly or ecstatic state of awareness. It is the intuitive sense of being connected to something greater than ourselves, of being part of something that is innately strong, good, and generous. It is experientially knowing what Saint Paul stated in Acts 17:28: "In God we live and move and have our being." Super-consciousness is characterized by peace, joy, clarity, truth, fearlessness, endurance, unity, compassion, courage, abundance, and love.

What does this have to do with prayer? The Kriya Yoga tradition teaches that there are two principal means of nurturing super-consciousness: meditation and prayer. They are the left and right lungs of the spiritual life! Prayer brings us into conscious contact with God and builds an infallible pathway to super-consciousness. I could not fully live a spiritual life or fulfill my God-given duties without *both* meditation and prayer.

Sometimes people ask me, "Why is prayer necessary? Isn't everything that happens the will of God?" Prayer is necessary precisely because *not* everything that happens is the will of God! God uses everything that happens without ever violating our free will to bring about our highest good. Prayer, then, is ultimately the process of aligning our will to the Divine Will. Prayer is not directing God, but opening our hearts to God's loving and wise direction. Humble, sincere prayer allows God's highest good to be unleashed within our lives.

At its deepest level, prayer is intimacy with God. Prayer is the joy of relationship. Prayer is God-communion. Prayer is loving God. Prayer is receiving God's love. Prayer is the very essence of super-consciousness. Here, Saint Francis of Assisi captures the beautiful efficacy of prayer: "If you, O servant of God, are upset, for any reason whatever, you should immediately rise up to prayer, and you should remain in the presence of the Most High Father for as long as it takes for him to restore you to the joy of your salvation."[110]

---

110. *365 St. Francis of Assisi*, 109.

Body, Mind and Spirit

To understand how prayer unfolds, it is helpful to have a yogic understanding of the human person. We all have a body, and the body is good, but we are more than our bodies. We all have a mind, and we need the mind in order to function in the world. The mind takes in information through the five senses, categorizes that information, and then stores it, consciously or unconsciously. It is important to understand that the mind is entirely linear; its function is to understand creation, but not the Creator. The mind can make inferences about God that are descriptively true, but it cannot directly experience God because God transcends linear categories. God is a mystery that can be endlessly known, not in and through the categories of the mind, but through the union of our spirit to God's Spirit.

What is our spirit? The human spirit is the non-physical, non-linear aspect of the human being and the most subtle and sensitive facet of our humanness. Our human spirit is meant to touch God's Spirit. Conscious contact with God always occurs within our spirit, wherein God's Spirit infuses our human spirit with light, grace, divine energy, and love. True prayer, deep prayer, is the marriage of our spirit to God's Spirit – and we experience this marriage intuitively, not intellectually.

In a manner of speaking, our spirit is the most precious gift that God has given us because it allows us to enter into communion with God. What we must understand, however, is it that the human spirit needs to be protected, nurtured, and developed. The human spirit is like soft wax, taking on the form or imprint of those things to which it is exposed. If we consistently open our spirit to violence, negativity, fear, and chaos, it becomes traumatized. The result of such trauma is that the human spirit loses its capacity to intuit God, and we end up living our lives as rational animals rather than as God's children.

So how do we care for our spirit? The answer is really very simple: good reading, time spent in nature, loving conversations, selfless service, moral living, a balance between work and rest, the avoidance of drama, meditation, and consistent periods of silent solitude. These activities take us beyond our personalities, stories, and habits, and into our interior depths, where we begin to make contact with our spirits. Our love for God awakens, our longing for God is stirred, and our most secret prayers begin to bubble up into our awareness. Yogananda tells us how we know whether or not we are caring for our spirits: "Do you know the signs that you have not gotten along with God? They are restlessness, unhappiness, and an uneasy conscience. But if you are getting along with God, your conscience is at rest, and you are drunk with inner happiness and contentment all the time. I have no other desire but to be in that happiness and to give those living waters of joy to whomever comes to me."[111]

I have a busy life. I have a full-time psychotherapy practice, I oversee The Assisi Institute, and I have a

---

111. Paramahansa Yogananga, *Journey to Self-Realization* (Los Angeles, CA: Self-Realization Fellowship, 1997), 135.

rich family life. In addition to meditating two or three hours daily, I need a day of absolute rest where I can just be without having to talk to anyone for long periods of time. During these occasions, I can actually feel God's Spirit lovingly pressing upon my spirit. Insight and wisdom come to me. My strength is renewed, and my spirit is refreshed!

The Process of Prayer

To begin with, we must learn the distinction between praying *to* God and praying *in* God. Praying to God is trying to get God's attention, as if God were distant or unconcerned with us. Praying in God naturally arises from a sense of loving closeness or intimacy. For this reason, Yogananda taught that the best time to pray is at the end of meditation because our hearts are opened, our spirits are tender, and there is a sense of being *with* or *in* God. When we pray in God, our prayers are transparent, authentic, and pure – which makes them more powerful. Yogananda tells us, "The average man prays to God with his mind only, not with all the fervor of his heart. Such prayers are too weak to bring any response. We should speak to the Divine Spirit with confidence and with the feeling of closeness, as to a father or mother."[112]

The goal of prayer is not to behave in a pious manner or to live up to some image of a saint or holy person. The goal of prayer is God-communion or super-consciousness. Therefore, we must be absolutely sin-

---

112. Paramahansa Yogananda, *How You Can Talk With God*, 8.

cere and real. We must bring all of who we are into our relationship with God. We must choose to be vulnerable if we desire prayerful communion with God. When we read *Autobiography of a Yogi*, we see that Yogananda expressed the full spectrum of human emotion to God, from love and joy to fear and anger.

Again, sincerity is the key. At any time of the day, no matter what we are doing, we can stop and consciously breathe. And then, it's a matter of speaking to God from the heart. If we need peace, we ask for peace. When we need guidance, strength, patience, or courage, we simply have to ask. Jesus said, "Seek and you shall find, ask and it shall be given to you; knock and the door will be opened to you."[113] Often, when I am in a situation that is uncomfortable or potentially confrontational, I will go within and ask God to make me an instrument of his peace. Without fail, guidance comes, and I intuitively know how to proceed.

Finally, we should never underestimate the power of prayerful gratitude. Such prayers open the heart and easily nurture a sense of conscious contact with God. When I sit to meditate in the morning, my very first act is to thank God for at least five blessings in my life. I always begin with thanking God for waking me up, for giving me one more day to love my family and for another opportunity to bring light into the world. After all, not everyone who goes to bed at night wakes up the next morning. Do I always feel grateful at the start of my prayers? No, but by making the choice to express gratitude to the Divine something in my spirit is touched, and the meditation that follows

---

113. Matthew 7:7.

tends to flow quite easily. If the only prayer we ever prayed was one of gratitude, that would be quite sufficient! A study shows that prayers of gratitude lesson anxiety and increase the flow of those biological chemicals that enhance our happiness and sense of well-being .[114]

Formal Prayers

In addition to those spontaneous prayers that simply emerge from our hearts, it is helpful to integrate traditional or ritual prayers into our prayer life. All too often, we waste a lot of energy reinventing the wheel! Our ancestral mothers and fathers have passed on to us prayers that have been inspired from above and act as magical pathways into the heart of God. Returning to the practice of traditional prayers is, in part, the meeting of the fifth commandment, "Honor thy mother and thy father."

My mother's passing provides a good example of ritualized prayer. She was not necessarily a strict Catholic, but during the week leading up to her death she prayed the rosary and again and again. When she grew too weak to continue on her own, my older sister prayed it with her. Undoubtedly, the rosary helped to make her transition peaceful.

I also rely on the rosary, particularly when I pray for people. I offer each bead or Hail Mary for a specific

---

114. Harvard Health Publications, "In Praise of Gratitude," November, 2011.
http://www.health.harvard.edu/newsletter_article/in-praise-of-gratitude.

person. In other situations, I may not have the words to pray, even though I need to pray. During these times, I will pray the Lord's Prayer or I will repeat the prayer of Jesus in the Garden of Gethsemane, "Not my will, but thy will be done." One of my favorite prayers is a simple mantra that Yogananda prayed, "God, Christ, Guru."

It is impossible to overstate the power or efficacy of these traditional prayers! When we pray them, our individual prayer joins the chorus of prayers that are being offered all over the world and in heaven by God's people. They are powerful! When we pray them with sincerity and purity, they bring us into conscious contact with God and put us in the flow of God's loving and all-powerful will.

Sometimes, one ritual prayer offered to God makes all the difference. At other times, we may have to offer our prayers to God over and over, as long as it takes to reestablish our conscious contact with God. It is important to note that prayer, whether we are feeling it or not, strengthens our spiritual will. The stronger our spiritual will is, the easier it is to make conscious contact with God. If we are persistent in prayer over time, we will find that our spirits are praying for us even when our minds and bodies are engaged in external activity, and the presence of God will become part and parcel of our general awareness. This is what St. Paul meant when he said, "Pray unceasingly."[115]

---

115. 1 Thessalonians 5:17.

The Prayer of Tears, Groaning, and Sighing

If prayer is making eye contact with God, a life of prayer is maintaining that eye contact, no matter what. Such intimacy, however, demands that we go deeper than our superficial personality and reach underneath our stories, words, and thoughts. In the depth of prayer, our spirits communicate with the Divine in groans, sighs, and tears, sometimes external and other times internal. I am not talking about a form of emotional piety, but a depth of communication that is beyond the mind, imagination, and emotions. What is actually happening is that God's Holy Spirit is pressing upon our spirit, and as a result we groan, sigh, or cry. We are, quite literally, being moved to tears. Thomas of Celano, a follower and biographer of St. Francis, wrote, "When Francis prayed in the wilds and in solitary places, he would fill the woods with sighs, water the earth with tears, beat his breast with his hand, and there, making the most of a more intimate, secret place, he often spoke aloud with his Lord."[116]

At the deepest level, this form of prayer is actually God's Spirit praying in us and through us. This prayer cannot be taught; it unfolds to the degree that we sincerely aspire to be one with God. It is as if God cracks open our spirits, and our intense love and longing for God reaches into God's very heart. We cannot make this kind of prayer happen; it comes as a gift or a grace, often unexpectedly. But when it comes, it has the power to move heaven and earth because it is God praying through us. In the words of St. Paul, "In the

---

116. *365 St. Francis of Assisi*, 118.

same way the Spirit also helps our weakness, for we do not know how to pray as we should, but the Spirit Himself intercedes for us with groanings too deep for words, and He who searches the heart knows what the mind of the Spirit is, because He intercedes for the saints according to the will of God."[117]

The Prayer of Silent Union

If we persevere in prayer, eventually God bestows a wonderful gift upon us: the prayer of silent union.[118] In the prayer of union, there are no thoughts, words, images, or efforts. God literally quiets the faculties of imagination and thinking and simply draws us into union with Himself, so much so that where God ends and we begin is not at all clear. It is as if we are in a state of deep, dreamless sleep, yet we are fully conscious. Just as a husband and wife become one in the act of love-making, our spirit and God's Spirit become one in love. It is as if God fully surrenders to us, which allows us to surrender to God in return. Sometimes the prayer of silent union will occur during meditation and at other times when we least expect it. For example, sometimes when I am gardening my heart will spontaneously open. Suddenly I am lost in the wonder of the moment and the silence. I actually lose a sense of myself.

We cannot maintain the intensity of this prayerful state in its purest form, but it leaves a permanent im-

---

117. Romans 8:26–27.
118. The prayer of silent union is equivalent to the Great Silence, only approached from a different direction. At the deepest level, prayer and meditation converge.

print on our spirit nevertheless. The prayer of union changes us: a clear sense of God's presence follows us into all of our activities, helping us to have a steady heart and a peaceful mind. Almost effortlessly, we stay away from anything that would drive a wedge between the sense of God's presence and ourselves. We naturally integrate a level of solitude into our lives because we desire to return to that simple and loving state of prayerful union with the Divine.

In all of these forms of prayer, what we eventually become aware of is that God not only *answers* our prayers, but *responds* to us personally! In other words, we discover that our prayer invokes an actual response from God and guru that we can literally sense or intuit. The more we perceive this response, the more we will want to pray, and super-consciousness or God-communion becomes a way of life. Yogananda tells us, "If once you can get that response you will never feel separated from God again. The divine experience will always remain with you. But that 'once' is difficult because the heart and mind are not convinced; doubt creeps in because of your previous materialistic beliefs."[119] We must use our spiritual will and a loving manner to push through our doubt and resistance.

Finally, we must ask, what do we pray about? And the answer is simple: everything! We must not seek to bring God only into our prayer life and our spirituality, but into our finances, our sexuality, our relationships, everything! I'm not suggesting that we throw common sense out the window or that we refuse to use logic in our decision-making. What I am saying is

---

119. Paramahansa Yogananda, *How You Can Talk With God*, 34.

that we must seek to divinize every aspect of our lives by surrendering all things to God.

A qualification can be helpful here. Many years ago, a wise spiritual mentor reminded me of something we don't like to think about much: obedience. He told me that if I really wanted God's guidance in the affairs of my life, I had to practice obedience. Obedience is the necessary pre-condition for receiving God's guidance. Otherwise, the arteries of our spiritual receptivity are clogged by our own willfulness. We only hear God's voice to the extent that we are willing to do whatever it is that God calls us to do. If we consciously or unconsciously limit what we will do or not do, we cannot hear anything outside of those limits. In prayer, Francis once heard Jesus imploring him to find God's presence in all people, regardless of their appearances. The following story captures Francis' lovingly obedient response:

> One day [Francis] was carrying stones down the hill from Assisi when a leper was approaching him on the trail. There was no way to avoid him. Francis was nervous. His whole life, he had always turned his head from anything remotely disturbing... Today something stopped his automatic response and he dared look. This leper was a man. He had a soul. Before Francis knew it, he had dropped his stones and run back up the hill toward the stranger...Francis found himself moving toward the leper, reaching for his face, and yes, kissing him on the lips. This man in that moment was God. And God was freeing Francis...For Francis, everything ugly was now and

forever a part of God's beauty.[120]

For me, obedience is not a natural virtue. By nature, I tend to be a bit oppositional. What I have come to understand is that my opposition or my resistance to obedience is rooted in fear. Can I trust God? The Truth? Reality? Love? To the extent that I can trust, my ability to obey increases. In short, obedience is not enslavement, but the willingness to listen with an open and vulnerable heart. The word obedience comes from the Latin *obedire*, which means not only "to obey" but also "to listen." Thus, obedience is not enslavement, but the willingness to listen with an open and vulnerable heart.

We have explored the nature of God, the practice of Kriya Yoga meditation, and prayer. But if our spiritual realizations are going to impact the quality of our lives, they must be stabilized within a healthy and holy lifestyle. In the next chapter we will look at what such a lifestyle entails.

---

120. Bruce Davis, *Simple Peace: The Spiritual Life of St. Francis of Assisi* (Lincoln, NE: Author's Choice Press, 2000), 8.

7 THE KRIYA LIFESTYLE

My first meditation teacher took me under his wing thirty years ago. Initially, his approach perplexed me. Before he would even begin to teach me a meditation technique, he made me commit to these practices: wake each day by 6 am and go to bed each night by 10 pm; take a walk every day; remain celibate for a period of time; eat less meat; and call him every morning. In one of those morning calls, he asked if I had made my bed. I snapped back, "Are you my mother?" He immediately hung up on me! When I called him the next morning, I quickly announced that I had made my bed. He answered, "Good; now you're ready to learn to meditate." In hindsight, it is clear that he was trying to teach me that there is a spectacular, infinitely wise precision embedded within the laws of nature and an order to all aspects of existence. The Book of Proverbs underscores the reality of this ever-present, ever-guiding wisdom: "Listen as Wisdom

calls out... I call to you, to all of you. I raise my voice
to all people. I, Wisdom, was appointed in ages past,
at the very first, before the earth began... I was there
when he established the heavens, when he drew the
horizon on the oceans... I was the architect at his
side, a master craftsman. I was his constant delight,
rejoicing always in his presence. And how happy I was
with the world he created; how I rejoiced with the
human family. Now, therefore, listen to me, my children, for blessed are those that keep my ways."[121]

Similarly, Yogananda tells us, "Every saint who has
penetrated to the core of Reality has testified that a
divine universal plan exists and that it is beautiful and
full of joy."[122] Creation is not a roll of the dice! The
very intelligence of God is embedded within creation
as a Guiding, Organizing, and Designing force. As we
begin to meditate, our nervous systems begin to let go
of stress and tension, and we begin to experience real
silence. The intelligence of God begins to consciously
awaken within us, not as intellectual information, but
as intuitive knowledge – what the Christian tradition
refers to as "enlightened conscience." As we meditate
we lose our rigidity, our fixations, and our obsessions.
Our psychological knots loosen. We become more
fluid. We become deeply sensitive to the movements
of grace, inspiration, and the Divine Mind. More and
more we are guided by an informed conscience, by inspired intuition, and by the guru's teachings. Therefore, as our silence, peace, and relaxation deepens and
we increasingly find ourselves in an ever-deepening

121. Prov. 8. The word "wisdom" is of the feminine gender in both Hebrew and Greek,
reminding us of the significance of the Divine Mother and Her presence in the ongoing
work of creation.
122. Paramahansa Yogananda, *Autobiography*, 420.

flow of God's grace-filled wisdom, we strive to live in a natural and integrated manner, as God intended us to live.

Yamas, Niyamas, Commandments, and Beatitudes

Every spiritual path has a set of guidelines for life. Yoga has its Niyamas (five rules of life) and Yamas (five qualities of observance); Judaism, the Ten Commandments; and Christianity, the Beatitudes. We can look at these injunctions as onerous rules handed down to us from oppressive patriarchal systems, or we can choose to see them as love letters from our Divine Parent, full of pure knowledge and care. Yogananda tells us, "He who would ensure his happiness and well-being and his ultimate arrival in the kingdom of supreme beatitude (bliss) must be neither a manipulator nor a scofflaw of those righteous ways."[123] To the degree that we enter into the Silence and realize our innate spiritual nature, we instinctively desire to live a balanced and harmonious life in alignment with God's natural order.

By prayerfully meditating on the niyamas, the yamas, the Ten Commandments, and the Beatitudes of Jesus, our intuitive desire to live a wholesome and holy life is given shape and form in the very same ways that have successfully guided spiritual seekers from time immemorial. I strongly suggest that you approach these love letters from God in a childlike spirit of wonder, curiosity, and openness. These righteous

---

123. Paramahansa Yogananda, *The Second Coming*, 457 – 458.

ways are not meant to induce toxic shame, but to awaken us to our true nature in the Divine Image. We do not serve them; they serve us as maps leading us in the direction of God-realization. This is what Jesus meant when he said, "The Sabbath was made for man, and not man for the Sabbath."[124]

NIYAMAS – FIVE RULES OF LIFE

Self Purification (Shaucha)

We come to God not as angels but as human beings – we have bodies and minds, and we live in a physical environment. If these containers are to hold God's light, they must be cleansed of impurities. We must care for our bodies, giving them proper rest, exercise, and food. Our living environment must be orderly and peaceful, filled with as much natural beauty as possible and always conducive to God's grace, to peace, to laughter, and to joy. At the level of the mind, we must work to keep our thoughts pure. Remember, thoughts are things; they are energy forms, and there is no such thing as neutral energy. Energy either strengthens or weakens us, paving the way for God-realization or reinforcing egoic consciousness. Many years ago, when I was in the presence of somebody I consider to be a saint, I made an off-color remark, trying to be funny. While others laughed, he glanced in my direction, briefly making eye contact with me. Later that night, he gave a talk about the importance of being pure-minded. I got the message!

---

124. Mark 2:27.

Contentment (Santosha)

Contentment is really a very simple practice: it is wanting only what we already have and not wanting what we don't have. It is a form of radical acceptance of self, others, and whatever life brings us. Though contentment certainly involves a psychological process, it is ultimately rooted in God's providence, which means that everything that comes to us serves our highest evolution and is in some mysterious way the very will of God. The great Jesuit spiritual director Jean-Pierre De Caussade says it best: "We must put all speculation aside and, with childlike willingness, accept all that God presents to us. What God arranges for us to experience at each moment is the best and holiest thing that could happen to us."[125] Such radical acceptance does not create passivity, but paradoxically opens us to discerning the will and guidance of God in any and all circumstances. Why? Because we are not resisting what is!

Self Discipline (Tapas)

As a young man, I played many sports. Athletes implicitly accept that success demands discipline, sacrifice, and a degree of self-denial – not because of any masochistic motivation, but because of a greater goal: the joys of teamwork, mastery, and success. Likewise, Yogananda encourages us to see ourselves as "spiritual athletes," guided by the "superior joys of an inner

---

125. Jean-Pierre De Caussade, *Abandonment to Divine Providence* (New York: Doubleday, 1975), 27.

heaven."[126] We are all filled with powerful currents of energy, including our sexual energy. The goal is not to demonize these drives, but to harness them, elevate them, and place them at the service of truth, beauty, and goodness, putting them at the disposal of God and our own souls. As our natural energies are divinized, we become powerful warriors in the service of all that is good. At a certain level, this is what Jesus meant when he said, "Blessed are the poor in spirit, for theirs is the kingdom of God."[127] In the spirit of Jesus' teaching, Yogananda tells us, "As a poor man is glad to discard his rags when he becomes rich, so the successful God-seeker, entering the world of bliss, jubilantly casts away all shabby material attachments."[128]

Self-Study (Svadhyaya)

What shapes our perceptions and values? The court of public opinion? Political perspectives? Social media? These are more than intellectual or theoretical questions. The way we view life – the way we interpret reality – determines the quality of our lives. Authentic scriptures such as the Judeo-Christian Bible and the Bhagavad Gita are inspired by the Holy Spirit and convey the very mind of God. They reflect a level of pure, inspired knowledge. When they are properly interpreted and applied to life they produce people like Francis of Assisi, Mother Teresa, Gandhi, Dorothy Day, and Paramahansa Yogananda. I doubt that the

---

126. Paramahansa Yogananda, *The Bhagavad Gita*, 960.
127. Matthew 5:3.
128. Paramahansa Yogananda, *The Bhagavad Gita*, 960.

New York Times or Facebook ever produced such evolutionary giants! What would our lives be like if each day we meditated and then quietly reflected on the words of scripture or of a great saint? The consciousness that gave birth to the words would penetrate into our very DNA, purifying our minds, transforming our emotions, and empowering our wills. Our lives would resonate with a divine and life-giving intensity. Jesus said, "Heaven and earth will pass away, but my words will never pass away."[129]

There is another necessary dimension of self-study. St John of the Cross said that next to knowledge of God, nothing is more important than the knowledge of ourselves. The wisdom gleaned from prayerfully studying the words of a saint or a spiritual master serves as a mirror which reveals us to ourselves and helps us to see into ourselves with fresh and discerning eyes. This kind of interior discrimination helps us to understand what motivates us and what we are creating in our day to day lives. Such self-knowledge liberates us to make choices that are in alignment with our highest and noblest aspirations. Many years ago a spiritual director pointed out my tendency for self-pity and stated that it was not a helpful trait. When I asked him how to combat this tendency, he replied, "Truth is the answer," and then he quoted from St. Paul: "All things work together for the good for those who love God and are called according to his purposes." He told me, "Craig, if it is true that everything that happens to you is for your highest good, then there is no place in your thoughts for self-pity." To this day, when I am tempted to feel sorry for my-

---

129. Luke 21:33.

self, I remember what I learned from him.

Surrender to God (Ishvara Pranidhana)

There is a fundamental truth to human existence: we become what we focus on, what we serve, and what we love. By surrendering to God, we serve "That" which is greater than ourselves. Surrender brings out our God-given greatness. For example, Francis of Assisi loved Jesus and sought to imitate him in all things. He surrendered everything to his Lord. Two years before he died, an angel appeared to Francis and pierced his body with the five wounds of the crucified Christ. In a manner of speaking, Francis became another Christ; he became what he loved. Jesus tells us, "Blessed are the pure in heart, for they shall see God."[130] To be pure of heart is to give up our infatuation with lesser gods, and in the words of Jesus, to "Love the Lord your God with all your heart, and with all your soul, and with all your strength, and with all your mind."[131] Such single-minded devotion leads to a level of concentration whereby we experience oneness, or Samadhi, with God. This means that we are able to see the glory of God in ourselves and in creation. The bottom line is that without this loving surrender to God, we cannot experience union with God.

---

130. Matthew 5:8.
131. Luke 10:27.

YAMAS – FIVE QUALITIES OF OBSERVANCE

Non-violence (Ahimsa)

Most of us do not think of ourselves as violent people, and thankfully this is true, at least on a physical level. But subtle levels of violence exist in our thoughts, words, and intentions, and spontaneous streams of violent feelings and impulses often arise in our minds. So long as we are unattached to them and can rise above them, they cause no harm. Rather than expending our energies fighting off violent tendencies, it is better to internalize these words of Jesus: "Love your neighbor as yourself."[132] This commandment to love others as ourselves has often been wrongly interpreted in a psychological sense, meaning that we can only love our neighbor as much as we love ourselves. This is not at all what Jesus meant! To the point, when through prayer and meditation we merge into God, into love, we experience the interconnectedness of all life-forms; we intuitively grasp the truth that we are all drinking from the same well of life. We see both our friends and our enemies as extensions of ourselves: as mothers and fathers, sons and daughters. To harm them is literally to harm ourselves! Once we grasp the oneness of creation, our tendency to do violence drops like dead fruit on a vibrant tree.

Truth (Satya)

Jesus tells us, "If you continue in my word, then you

132. Mark 12:31.

are my disciples indeed; and you shall know the truth and the truth shall set you free."[133] The truth that Jesus speaks of transcends the limitations of dogmas and creeds. Rather, it is a living truth that unfolds in the context of a loving relationship with God and guru. Ultimately, Jesus is speaking of the truth of who we are in God. This means that we are only free when we live from the soul, the Self. Otherwise, we are driven by the blind forces of karma, habit, and ignorance. Yogananda paraphrased Jesus' words in this way: "If you persist in attunement with the Cosmic Vibration (the Holy Spirit) as heard in meditation and with the Christ Consciousness...then indeed you may consider yourselves my disciples, disciplined and guided by my word or the Christ Intelligence within you. By this you will be able to know all truth – about yourself, the mysteries of life, and the drama of the cosmos. You will no longer identify with human desires and the consequent bondage of karma, thereby freeing yourself from delusion and reincarnations."[134]

Non-stealing (Asteya)

On the surface, the practice of non-stealing appears simple and straightforward. On a deeper level, however, it is much more challenging. It is the choice to share our abundance with others, and not to devour what we don't need. This is not a veiled reference to socialism, but to the natural generativity that springs from the heart of a person who has realized his or her

133. John 8:32.
134. Paramahansa Yogananda, *The Second Coming*, 998 – 990.

essential oneness with all of humanity. As our hearts expand we naturally begin to experience others as an extension of ourselves, whether or not they belong to our religious and racial tribes. Jesus tells us, "Anyone who has two shirts should share with the one who has none, and anyone who has food should do the same."[135]

Chastity (Brahmacharya)

The goal of the spiritual life is not the repression of our natural energies, but the divinization of those energies, including our sexual energy. When our sexual energy is not brought to the level of the heart center, it remains an animalistic instinct and tends to control us, bringing chaos and confusion into our lives. But when through the practice of pranayama, meditation, and devotion the sexual energy is infused with the force of divine love, we become more alive, more generative, and more creative. Both Yogananda and Mother Teresa were consecrated celibates, yet they birthed great spiritual families and breathed much life into the world. Their sexual energy was very fruitful on a much higher and more expansive level because it was entirely divinized. Many years ago, a wise spiritual mentor gave me this advice: "Don't write a check with your body that your life can't cash."[136] He was trying to teach me that sex outside of a truly committed, loving relationship typically brings suffering to one or both partners. By contrast, when sex is an ex-

---

135. Luke 3:11.
136. Richard Rohr said these words to me, and I have said them to many others since then.

pression of selfless devotion, fidelity, and love, it nurtures the relationship, deepens the marital bond, brings a shared joy to the couple, and potentially begets life.

Non-grasping (Aparigraha)

Most of us are in the grasp of something: desires, attachments, compulsions, obsessions, addictions, aversions, regrets, fears, and so forth. On our own, we are incapable of freeing ourselves from these forces that appear to hold us hostage. But as we come into contact with a Higher Power, these forces begin to lose their grip on our lives. Our job is to continue our spiritual practices with steadfast devotion, because we can only relinquish our grasping to the extent that we are experiencing God's presence, grace, and love. For this reason, the silence born of meditation is essential. Such silence not only quiets our noisy minds, but it brings an interior richness to our spirit which liberates us from our attachment to inferior forms of happiness. Authentic spirituality is not a denial of the goodness of creation, but the willingness to seek the highest happiness, the highest beauty, and the highest good. Within all desires, even those so-called lesser desires, is the desire for God. The goal, therefore, is not to deny our desires, but to direct them to the one great all-fulfilling desire – union with God. This is true renunciation!

One could easily interpret the yamas and niyamas as recipes for earning God's love. Nothing could be farther from the truth! God is simple. God is love. God only loves, without regard for our holiness or lack of it! These sacred prescriptions open our spiritual arteries so that God's lifeblood can more easily flow in and through our hearts. They prepare us for the experience of God's liberating presence and then help us to stabilize that presence.

THE FRUITS OF SPIRITUAL PRACTICE

As we endeavor to live our lives according to these sacred prescriptions, blesssings necessarily appear. Earlier, we looked at the natural progression of the spiritual life according to Kriya Yoga tradition: Self-realization, Christ Consciousness, and God-realization. Now, let's look at how the process of the spiritual life unfolds. Yogananda names this process in this way: *dharana (concentration) leads to dhyana (contemplation), and dhyana ultimately leads to Samadhi (union)*.[137] This is the process that leads to Self-realization, Christ Consciousness, and God-realization.

Concentration (Dharana)

The first blessing or fruit of meditation and right lifestyle is the art of concentration, or what yogis refer to as "dharana." If we are honest with ourselves, we will readily admit that our will, imagination, and emo-

---

137. This progression parallels St. Bonaventure's way of purification (concentration), illumination (contemplation), and union (samadhi).

tional energies are often captivated by something other than God; we tend to suffer from a kind of spiritual Attention Deficit Disorder. This is why we don't experience God's presence consistently. Our attention is scattered by our attachments and our aversions. The truth of the matter is that God is everywhere, hiding in plain sight. Becoming aware of God's presence is the simple process of focusing our attention on God and holding our focus in such a way that we become more deeply aware of God's presence. For example, before I began to write this morning I had to water our garden. I was tight for time, so I grumbled at having to fit in this chore. As I watered my beloved fig trees, I decided to be grateful to God for the beauty of the vegetation all around me. Immediately, I became aware of the one breath of life permeating me and the many beautiful plants, flowers, and trees that surrounded me. My irritated mood easily morphed into a simple, wakeful joy, all because I chose to shift my attention from a negative to a positive perception.

Every time we make the choice to pray, to meditate, to offer our lives to God as a living sacrifice, our spiritual will aligns with the gravitational pull of God's will. This alignment divinizes and strengthens our will, making it easier to nurture our capacity for single-minded concentration. Yogic concentration is not a tension-filled tug of war with the mind or imagination, but the movement of one's heart and soul toward ever deepening perceptions of the divine life. What does this look like? We are more and more involved in everything we do with a lively alertness and a keen wakefulness. We are increasingly spontaneous while drawing from an unseen well of intelligence. We are open to a spectrum of experience, including both deep sorrow and profound joy. Effortless concentration, a sense of playful lightness, and a growing level of stabilized silence become the bedrock of our day-to-day experiences. Valentin Tomberg describes it this way: "The changing of work, which is duty, into play, is effected as a consequence of the presence of the 'zone of perpetual silence,' where one draws from a sort of secret and intimate respiration, whose sweetness and freshness accomplishes the anointing of work and transforms it into play.'[138]

Spiritual concentration is much like using a magnifying glass to take the disperse rays of the sun and focus them into a single, intense ray. Concentration is a purifying of our attention through the loving use of our will. We cannot get any closer to God until we are focused. When we make a choice out of love to focus more and more of the rays of our attention on God, we are naturally led into contemplation, where we are able to intuit God's all-pervading presence within reality as it is.

Contemplation (Dhyana)

We have already discussed the act of contemplation.[139] Now let's look at a deeper level of this essential practice. Yogananda tells a story of an incident that took

---

138. Tomberg, *Meditations on the Tarot*, 11.
139. See the chapter on Kriya Yoga Meditation.

place with his guru, Sri Yukteswar, that captures the relationship between concentration and enlightened contemplation. While Sri Yukteswar was expounding on the sacred scriptures, Yogananda's mind apparently meandered into a future project. Immediately, Sri Yukteswar called this lapse to Yogananda's attention, saying, "You are not here.... The subtle truths I am expounding cannot be grasped without your complete concentration."[140]

Concentration leads to contemplation. So let us examine once again what contemplation is. Contemplation is not analysis, speculation, or the scrutiny of facts. No! Contemplation is the direct and intuitive experience of truth, the truth of existence as it is and not what we want the truth to be. It is the capacity to grasp reality, to taste reality, to be pulled into the really real. Contemplation is the willingness to be completely present to what is, to the suchness of life, with a kind of naked intent. For example, a theologian might know *about* God, but the contemplative *knows* God in an immediate sense because he or she is absolutely present to God as God is. Here, Lahiri Mahasaya says it perfectly: "Clear your mind of dogmatic theological debris; let in the fresh, healing waters of direct perception. Attune yourself to the active inner Guidance; the Divine Voice has the answer to every dilemma of life."[141]

We can read about the beauty of a pristine forest, we can view photos of this natural wonder, and we can even imagine what it would be like to hike in that

---

140. Paramahansa Yogananda, *Autobiography*, 101.
141. Ibid., 285.

forest. But nothing actually compares to being there, to experiencing the actual sights, sounds, and smells of the forest. Thomas Aquinas was a saint and much revered Catholic theologian from the 13th century. To this day, his writings undergird much of the Church's theological understanding. Unexpectedly, Thomas underwent a mystical experience that he was incapable of putting into words. Afterwards he said, "I will write no more. Everything that I have written seems like straw." And he never wrote again.

Recently, someone asked me, "Do you really believe in God?"

I surprised him when I answered, "No, I don't believe in God."

He asked, "So how can you teach others to meditate in order to find God?"

I replied, "I don't believe in God, because I experience God as a living reality. I know that I am known by God."

It is important to note that as we contemplate truth experientially, our mental and emotional lives become clearer, more peaceful, and richer. Jesus tells us, "You shall know the truth and the truth shall set you free."[142]

Through contemplation, our attention is purified and focused on God. We are receptive to reality as it is, and we find truth to be a purifying and healing

---

142. John 8:32.

balm. In this state, we become united with the reality of God. We enter into union.

Union (Samadhi)

My first meditation teacher repeatedly told me, "If you hang around a house of prostitution you are going to become a sex addict. If you hang around a barbershop you're going to get a haircut. If you hang around saints, you will become a saint. It's that simple." In other words, *concentration leads to contemplation, and contemplation leads to union.* Union is the process of becoming one with the object of our contemplation, with God. The experience of union moves us beyond our illusion of separateness and beyond the prison of isolation. As we contemplate the Divine by attentively sitting at the feet of the guru and becoming absorbed in truth, beauty, and goodness, our consciousness literally becomes a participation in God's consciousness. This how we are meant to live – in conscious communion with God!

At first, our union with God takes form as peace, as the Aum vibration, as light, as a sense of personal presence, as loving devotion to the guru, and so forth. But these wonderful aspects of God are still only partial. There is a deeper, total, and unfathomable level of union with God – the Great Silence. It is important to note what the Great Silence is not: it is not merely being quiet, not only the absence of external noise, and certainly not the ego wrestling the noisy mind into submission. Rather, the Great Silence is a state of consciousness that naturally occurs when we open ourselves to God's presence. Ultimately, the Great Silence descends as a gift, as grace. We cannot force it with techniques or invite it with our good behavior or piety. It is only emptiness, interior poverty, and surrender that can make us ready for the experience of the Great Silence. Yogi Sri Aurobindo, a contemporary of Yogananda, tells us, "It is not easy to get into the Silence... It is easier to let the Silence descend into you... It is to remain quiet at the time of meditation, not fighting with the mind or making mental efforts to pull down the Power of the Silence, but keeping a silent will and aspiration for them."[143]

The Great Silence is the presence of God beyond any image or concept; it is beyond the feeling of devotion, beyond dogma, beyond perspective, beyond anything personal. Teresa of Avila tells us that as the Great Silence descends, "God strikes the soul blind and deaf."[144] In other words, God suspends our capacity to think thoughts, to imagine, and to desire, yet we remain fully conscious, awake, and present. According to Teresa, "God unites himself with her, with the soul, and she understands nothing. She loses her senses and her reason entirely... it is impossible to say anything more that could be understood with words, except that the soul – I mean the spirit of the soul – is made one with God, Who is also spirit...all that God wants is to be joined with his creatures so completely that they can never be torn apart... Spiritual marriage is like a bright light pouring into a room from two large windows: it enters from different places, but be-

---

143. Madhav Pundalik Pandit, *Dictionary of Sri Auribindo's Yoga* (Twin Lakes, WI: Lotus Light Publications, 1992), 234.
144. St. Teresa of Avila, *The Interior Castle*, trans. Miribai Starr (New York: Riverhead Books, 2003), 263.

comes one light."[145]

The intense experience of union, *Samadhi*, cannot be maintained perpetually, moment by moment, but can become the backdrop of our everyday experience and the context in which we live even the most mundane aspects of our lives. The Great Silence supports all of our endeavors, inspires all of our actions, and guides every detail of our lives with loving precision. Where we end and God begins is not clear at all. We live from the stabilized consciousness of loving union. Yogananda refers to this state as *Nirvakalpa Samadi*, living our lives within the consciousness of loving union with God: "He (the Yogi) communes with God...in his ordinary waking consciousness, even in the midst of exacting worldly duties."[146]

Union is Always a Gift

Once again, we must remember that we cannot make the experience of union happen; it is always a gift, a gift that the Divine Mother desires to give all of her children. Furthermore, if we experienced absolute union with God without proper preparation, we would not be able to remain in the body! All of the practices of Kriya Yoga, the discipline of the Yamas and Niyamas, and a strong relationship with the guru help to integrate the experience of God-realization into our nervous systems, our psyches, and our everyday lives. We only need to know that every prayer, every medi-

---

145. Ibid., 270.
146. Paramahansa Yogananda, *The Second Coming*, 1590.

tation, every expression of devotion, and every act of loving service prepares us for the inevitable experience of absolute oneness with our Divine Beloved.

THE LAST WORD

We are living in troubling times. Everywhere we turn we seem to encounter cultural, political, racial, and religious strife. We want peace, but peace cannot happen when we are drunk with ideology, anger, and fear. So we wonder, is peace merely the absence of conflict? What is the substance of peace? Is peace little more than an idea?

I contend that true peace is the fruit of the energy of divine love, which helps us to see and experience our interconnectedness in God. To the degree that we recognize both our neighbors and our enemies as extensions of ourselves, we will naturally build bridges instead of walls, we will instinctively bear each other's suffering, and we will effortlessly strive to build a just society.

Here is the essential question: are we willing to look

beyond ourselves to a Higher Power so that we may transcend our individual and collective madness? We cannot free ourselves from the quicksand of the illusion of separateness by merely pulling up on our own ponytails. As Albert Einstein said, "No problem can be solved from the same consciousness that created it." A higher consciousness is needed. Psalm 69:1-2 perfectly expresses our predicament:

> Save me, O God!
> For the waters have come
> Up to my neck.
> I sink in deep mire,
> Where there is no foothold;
> I have come into deep waters,
> And the flood sweeps over me.

We do not need the unleashing of angry, irrational forces or dark magic, and we need something greater than our own imaginative capacities, or personal magic. We need *sacred magic*. Sacred magic avails us of a power greater than ourselves – the energy of God's love – which is the only force capable of healing our blindness and restoring us to sanity.

Kriya Yoga stands in the rich and varied tradition of sacred magic, as do the mystical streams associated with Hinduism, Judaism, Christianity, Sufism, and so forth. Kriya Yoga is a path that teaches us how to co-operate with the energy of grace so that we can live as God intended us to live.

Kriya Yoga is magical in that it brings us into conscious and immediate contact with the Divine. In turn, we realize our actual our identity in God: God's

being-ness is also our being-ness, and we are insepa-
rably one with God. All the disciplines and practices
of Kriya Yoga serve one ultimate purpose: to bring us
into the experience of our oneness with God, or what
we refer to as mystical union. Without this mystical
element, religion tends to be reduced to beliefs, rituals, and laws, offering no transforming grace or power
to move us beyond our fractured state of consciousness.

The magic of Kriya Yoga, however, does not end with
only the experience of mystical union. I say this because mystical union bestows upon us inspired knowledge, or enlightenment. As enlightened beings, we
will know that we are more than the body, more than
the personality, and more than our stories. We will
know the inherent dignity of being God's "image,"
the bliss of being a spark of divine light, and the freedom of being a child of the Creator. We will be like
God, not apart from God, but with God, in God, and
because of God.

While this sacred knowledge born of mystical union
reveals us to ourselves, it also opens our eyes and
hearts to others. We will know that we are all part of
one tribe, drawing life from the same source. We will
know that we are all brothers and sisters and that
when one of us suffers, we all suffer. We will know
that we are one, without a loss of our individuality.
Once we experience this truth, no one will have to tell
us to be generous, to care for those who suffer, or to
bear the burdens of others. Why? Because we will
know, experientially, that everyone is an extension of
us. And as we instinctively care for ourselves, we will

also care for others – whether or not they share our religion, our ethnicity, or our ideology.

Finally, the magic of Kriya Yoga will empower us to express our God-given divinity within the context of our day-to-day lives. Our lives and our choices will become increasingly guided by a higher wisdom, which is the very Spirit of God. Jesus tells us, "When the Spirit of truth comes, he will guide you into all the truth, for he will not speak on his own authority, but whatever he hears he will speak, and he will declare to you the things that are to come."[147] In other words, our lives will become a force for healing and liberation. When the disciples of John the Baptist approached Jesus on John's behalf to learn if Jesus was the Messiah, Jesus told them, "Go and tell John what you have seen and heard: the blind receive their sight, the lame walk, lepers are cleansed, the deaf hear, and the poor have the good news preached to them."[148]

When I reflect on the life of Yogananda, I see a life that perfectly embodied Jesus' teachings. Yogananda was not a mystic lost in ecstasy, but a man whose mystical realizations empowered him to serve as a humanitarian, a healer, a force for societal change, a unifier of different religious traditions, an avatar, and a spiritual father to countless individuals. Even though Yogananda left the body over 60 years ago, his life and consciousness continue to be a transforming force in the world. He is our older evolutionary brother, showing us what we are all capable of becoming: the marriage of heaven and earth.

---

147. John 16:13.
148. Luke 7:21–22.

After reading Yogananda's autobiography, however, one might be tempted to think that his life was filled with nothing but extraordinary occurrences, a continuous flow of spellbinding miracles. Yes, the miraculous was evident in his life. But to become fixated on the sensational is a misreading of Yogananda's life and a misunderstanding of the nature of mysticism. Mysticism is about recognizing God in mundane, ordinary, everyday events. We don't meditate to be swept away in ecstasy, but that our eyes might be opened, enabling us to see God's presence everywhere – even in ourselves. But the opening of our eyes does not happen overnight. The scales that blind us only fall away after many tears of purification have been shed. If we dare to persevere in meditation, silence, and longing, we will see God everywhere, and we will know a truly ineffable joy. We will pray without praying, meditate without meditating, and worship without worshipping. We will finally be ourselves – not the self we thought ourselves to be, but the Self that has been hidden in God from the very beginning of time.

I will end this book with the story of Yogananda's first meeting with his beloved guru, Sri Yukteswar. Like so many of us, Yogananda began his spiritual journey with questions, searching, and a deep hunger for God. In a simple but profound way, this meeting captures the essence of the mystical life and shows what it means to be a lover of God.

Torn by spiritual anguish, I entered the attic one dawn, resolved to pray until an answer was vouchsafed. "Merciful Mother of the Universe, teach me Thyself through visions, or through a guru sent by Thee!"

The passing hours found my sobbing pleas without response, when suddenly I felt lifted as though bodily to a sphere uncircumscribed. "Thy Master cometh today!" A divine womanly voice came from everywhere and nowhere.

...As Habu and I moved on, I turned my head to survey a narrow, inconspicuous lane. A Christlike man in the ocher robes of a swami stood motionless at the end of the lane. ...A few eager steps and I was at his feet.

"Gurudeva!"

"Oh my own, you have come to me!" My guru uttered the words again and again in Bengali, his voice tremulous with joy. "How many years I have waited for you!... I shall give you my hermitages and all I possess."

"Sir, I come for wisdom and God-realization. Those are your treasure troves I am after!"

The swift Indian twilight had dropped its half-curtain before my master spoke again. His eyes held unfathomable tenderness. "I give you my unconditional love. Will you give me the same unconditional love?"

"I will love you eternally, Gurudeva!"

[My master replied,] "Ordinary love is selfish,

darkly rooted in desires and satisfactions. Divine love is without condition, without boundary, without change. The flux of the human heart is gone forever at the transfixing touch of pure love."[149]

I pray that you know in every fiber of your being that God is real, that Jesus is real, that Yogananda and the gurus are real, and that God's grace is real. I pray that you know that your life is a participation in the divine life and that you have always been in God and always will be in God. I pray that you know that you come from love, that you were created for love, and that your deepest nature is love. Finally, I pray that you know that you are one with God, one with all of God's children, and one with your own soul. Amen!

149. Paramahansa Yogananda, *Autobiography*, 78-80.

BIBLIOGRAPHY

Almass, A.H. *The Pearl Beyond Price*. Boston: Shambala, 2001.

Arnold, Christie. "A Lesson from Mother Teresa." thepapist.org/a-lesson-from-mother-teresa/.

Davis, Bruce. *Simple Peace: The Spiritual Life of St. Francis of Assisi*. Lincoln, NE: Author's Choice Press, 2000.

DeCaussade, Jean-Pierre. *Abandonment to Divine Providence*. New York: Doubleday, 1975.

Harvard Health Publications. "In Praise of Gratitude." November, 2011. http://www.health.harvard.edu/newsletter-article/in-praise-of-gratitude.

Leloup, Jean-Yves. *Being Still: Reflections on an Ancient Mystical Tradition*. Translated by M.S.Laird. New York: Paulist Press, 2003.

Pandit, Madhav Pundalik. *Dictionary of Sri Auribindo's Yoga*. Twin Lakes, WI: Lotus Light Publications, 1992.

Paramahamsa Prajnanananda. *Lahiri Mahasaya: Fountainhead of Kriya Yoga*. Vienna, Austria: Prajna Publication, 2009.

Paramahansa Yogananda. *How You Can Talk With*

God. Los Angeles: Self-Realization Fellowship, 1957.

_____. *Whispers From Eternity*. Los Angeles: Self-Realization Fellowship, 1986.

_____. *Journey to Self-Realization*. Los Angeles: Self-Realization Fellowship, 1997.

_____. *God Talks With Arjuna: The Bhagavad Gita*, 2nd ed. Los Angeles: Self-Realization Fellowship, 1999.

_____. *The Divine Romance*. 2nd Edition. Los Angeles: Self-Realization Fellowship, 2000.

_____. *Man's Eternal Quest*. Los Angeles: Self-Realization Fellowship, 2002.

_____. *The Second Coming of Christ*. Los Angeles: Self-Realization Fellowship, 2004.

_____. *Autobiography of a Yogi*. 13th Edition. Los Angeles: Self-Realization Fellowship, 2010.

Paulson, Norman. *Sacred Science: Meditation, Transformation, Illumination*. Buellton, CA: The Solar Logos Foundation, 1998.

Rajarsi Janakananda: A Great Western Yogi. Los Angeles: Self-Realization Fellowship, 1994.

Rohr, Richard. "What You Seek Is What You Are." cac.org/what-you-seek-is-what-you-are-2016-01-03/.

_____. "Completing The Divine Circuit." cac.org/completing-the-divine-circuit-2017-08-10/.

St. Bonaventure. *The Journey of the Mind to God.* Translated by Philotheus Boehner. Indianapolis: Hackett Publishing Company, 1993.

St. Teresa of Avila. *The Interior Castle.* Translated by Miribai Starr. New York: Riverhead Books, 2003.

Sri Yukteswar. *The Holy Science.* 8th Edition. Los Angeles: Self-Realization Fellowship, 1990.

Teilhard de Chardin, Pierre. *The Divine Milieu.* New York: HarperCollins Publishers, 2001.

365 St.Francis of Assisi. Translated by Murray Bodo. London: Fount, 1987.

Tomberg, Valentin. *Meditations on the Tarot.* New York: Penguin Group, 1985.

_____. *Inner Development.* Great Barrington, MA: Anthroposophic Press, 1992.

_____. *Lazarus Come Forth!* Great Barrington, MA: Lindisfarne Books, 2006.

THE AUTHOR

Isha Das (Craig Bullock) is the founder and spiritual director of The Assisi Institute. An ordained Kriya Yoga teacher with the Center for Spiritual Awareness, Isha Das is an accomplished writer, international lecturer and psychotherapist. Isha Das earned his graduate degrees in Theology from the University of Notre Dame and in Clinical Psychology from the University of Duquesne. His diverse education includes extensive study in psychology, spirituality, mysticism, world religions, and yoga.

OTHER BOOKS BY ISHA DAS
(CRAIG BULLOCK)

Living Grace: A Daily Companion for Meditation and Contemplation

Extravagant Love: Reflections of a Catholic Yogi

The Path to Healing: Experiencing God as Love

Living in the Heart of the Divine:
Prayers of Passion, Surrender & Love

THE ASSISI INSTITUTE

The Assisi Institute is dedicated to supporting individuals who seek a deeper relationship with God. Through the harmonious integration of Kriya Yoga and mystical Christianity, we are nurturing a sacred community of meditation, contemplative inquiry and compassionate living.

For more information, please visit:
www.assisi-institute.org

Made in the USA
Lexington, KY
13 July 2018